REDEMPTION ROAD

NOBODY COUNTED ON THE FELON

REDEMPTION ROAD

by

John A Galeotto

Norfolk
Publishing
Group

Norfolk Publishing Group
800 Boylston Street
Boston, MA 02199
www.npgbooks.com
info@npgbooks.com
editorial@npgbooks.com

Redemption Road
A Norfolk Publishing Group Book

NPG eBook Edition / November 2022
NPG Paperback Edition / November 2022
NPG Trade Hardback Edition / November 2022

Hardcover: ISBN 13: 978-1-950457-06-9 (Casebound w/jacket0
Hardcover: ISBN 13: 978-1-950457-08-3 (Casebound)
Paperback: ISBN 13: 978-1-950457-07-6

LCN:

Cover by Covers by Christian
www.coversbychristian.com

Interior design by Chris DiRusso
www.chris-dirusso.com

BVC: EB0P254V02T7076

John Galeotto Fan Mail: j.galeotto@npgbooks.com

To Shelli and Tim Adams
whose
encouragement and support
made
this novel possible

1

RELEASE

The gate didn't clang shut ominously behind him. In fact, there wasn't a gate at all. A regular door with a standard knob closed behind him as the guards escorted him to the van. However, he spent the better part of a decade behind a cement wall, excluded from society. He gazed out the window and watched as the prison shrank. The farther away they traveled, the more he hoped his old life would stay behind in the distance.

Mark Toren was far from perfect and had no delusions about the subject. The road to redemption would be a difficult one to travel. Of this, he had no doubt. None whatsoever. Life was too precious to worry about the past.

The transport officer stopped at a small convenience store five minutes later and told Mark to go in, get his ticket, come right out, and not linger in the store or buy anything else. Mark went in and came right out and got back in the van. The driver drove across the street to the commuter rail station and drove up to the platform. Here you go," he said. "Good luck."

"Thanks, I'll need it, that's for sure," Mark said as he got out.

The other guard got out and walked with him to the train to make sure he got onboard.

After taking a big deep breath of free air, Mark boarded the train and found a seat. The train lurched, then rolled onward. The conductor came around, and he handed him his ticket. He watched the DOC van pull off and leave the lot from the window of the train.

They had to wait for him to get on the train and for the train to start moving before they could leave. Yet, he could get off at the next stop and come right back. It made no sense to him, but it was one of the concessions the prison made with the town.

It felt weird to be free.

Mark couldn't wait to get to South Station and see Boston again. They stripped one's ability to do whatever one wanted to do while incarcerated, so everything was new to him. He watched the scenery pass by his window. Mesmerized by all the things he once took for granted. Soon. Mark would be home. *Home.* Back in his old stomping grounds.

With the human cattle packed in as tight as possible, Mark felt blessed to get a table seat where no one sat. Businesspeople walked past him and squeezed into other seats. A couple of people glared at him and gave him a dirty look. He figured they were regulars, and he took their seat. Most of the people were on their way to work. There was also a mix of kids of different ages who he assumed were on their way to school. College-aged kids were thrown in for good measure—an eclectic assortment of ethnicities. He felt out of place. Their reaction to him didn't help. Reality was slow to kick in. Like moving through a dream—though fully conscious. *Free*. Finally. *Free*.

The landscape changed from suburban to urban sprawl. The closer the train moved toward Boston, the more comfortable he became. Apprehension mixed with disbelief was something all returning citizens dealt with upon release. It may sound strange, but several years in prison could make a person afraid of society...and freedom. A new kind of strange. Most of all, he feared being held back for no other reason but something he did years prior. Luckily, Mark knew about the mental game the mind played.

As the train slowed to enter the next station, the car swayed from side to side. Only two more to go. Half the people in the train car where he sat debarked. Only to be replaced by a lot more students. The current group of kids wore similar clothing that matched. A private school, perhaps. Pants for the boys and skirts for the girls. Blue sweaters and tan chinos. The outfits screamed private school. Expensive and exclusive.

He scanned the faces of each newcomer—a habit from years in prison. The purpose was to spot any possible sign of trouble before it happened. He found nothing out of the ordinary—just mischievous shenanigans of the middle and high school variety. The train started to roll, and he felt at ease again.

Although Mark didn't have much of a plan, finding a job held the highest priority. He'd shack up at some rooming house until he could afford something better. The prison issued him a check, which had to be cashed or deposited. and $70 in cash He'd been able to save a little more than $3000, and if he budgeted carefully, he'd be okay for a couple of months. At least, he hoped. It all hinged on whether he could find a job in such a short time. Most people, even though desperate, wouldn't work for minimum wage. He had no problem with a low-wage job, although it wouldn't cover room and board. He'd take any job that helped stretch out the money he had saved and didn't care what he'd be doing in said job. As long as the job was legal, he'd give it a try.

He continued to stare out the window. The gray sky, with its thick dark clouds, rolled overhead. The surrounding scenery told him Boston was getting closer. Trees were replaced by concrete. The teenagers, who boarded at the last stop, were loud and obnoxious. They threw paper at each other and talked shit—typical teenagers.

Too much commotion for Mark that he thought about moving his seat but decided to give it a chance. He wasn't used to so many people around him. He tried his best to take his mind off all the possible challenges he would soon face.

Since he wanted to live outside the old neighborhood, he knew his criminal record would make finding a place difficult. He planned to avoid all temptation and couldn't go back to his old way of making money—it just wasn't worth the trouble. A man passed by him, which grabbed his attention. He noticed the man had a slight limp, which gave him a confident, smooth stride. Mark didn't see the man's face; however, he remembered the man boarding at the last stop. Though Mark thought the man had a backpack, he must've left it back on his seat. Brave man. Mark wouldn't leave his comb on the seat for fear it would be stolen.

The man with a limp was soon forgotten when a balled-up piece of paper hit him in the side of the face with a loud smack. Immediately, he stood, heated, and searched for the perpetrator. A teenager about 16 years old sheepishly apologized.

"No problem," Mark said in a low voice as he gathered his belongings and moved to the next car. At the moment, the kids were too much for him. The next train car forward was also a double. The bottom section was full, but to his surprise, upstairs had many empty seats. He found one in the middle—another seat with a table. There was another table on the other side, just like the last car. He sat down and exhaled a sigh of relief. Silence. So much quieter he could hear himself think.

A kid, perhaps twelve or thirteen, approached from the opposite direction. He stopped at the table. "Excuse me, sir," he said, motioning to the empty seat, "Is anyone sitting there?"

"No," Mark said, in his *and I had rather like it that way* tone. "Go ahead…all yours."

"Thanks," he said as he sat down, pulled out a laptop, and started typing.

Mark believed he was finishing up some homework before he got to school. The tapping of the keyboard was far less annoying than the kids in the other car.

"Last-minute homework?" Mark said, looking for a distraction from his worries.

"Yeah," the kid said. "A history report…boring too!"

Mark smiled as he resumed watching the scenery pass.

2

FIRST ATTACK

The murky gray sky disappeared as they went underground. The train rolled into the last stop before South Station— Back Bay. Mark watched the people around him and studied their facial expressions. The ability to read people was the only positive thing from his old life. The ability kept him alive in prison. And away from fools. With this stop's exchange complete, the train started to roll again.

As the other passengers took their seats, Mark stared out the window at the people milling about on the platform. Mark saw the man who passed him on the way to the laboratory. Something about the guy made him nervous. Mark could now see his face. Something was off. Then it came to him. The man didn't have his backpack, and he smiled oddly. The train rolled on. Mark blinked, and the man was gone. Hackles rose at the back of his neck. The train lurched and rolled forward as it exited the tunnel. Maybe he was just imag—

An explosion rocked the train. Mark acted purely on instinct as he ducked under the table, pulling the kid underneath with him. Heat rushed through the car as metal twisted and ripped apart the train. Debris landed everywhere. The ights went out. He wasn't sure what happened. *Darkness.*

The kid moaned and whispered something indiscernible. Mark had shielded him from the blast and twisting metal of the train as debris landed atop the table and blocked out all light.

"We gonna be all right?" The kid said in a shaky voice.

"Are you hurt?"

"No, I don't think so."

"Good, now let's get out of here," Mark said as he pushed on the debris around him, looking for a way out.

As he fumbled in the darkness, something moved. A crack of light broke through, easing his emotional state. His immediate concern was for that of the child, so he tried again and pushed harder. More light came into the cramped space. The object he'd been pushing on was the back of one of the seats. After a bit of struggle, Mark made enough room to crawl out.

The kid made no sound, and Mark couldn't see his facial expression in the limited light. However, he figured the kid was in shock. He had to get them out of there. Mark crawled out from the rubble first. A quick scan of the train car confirmed his fears. Blood splatter covered most of the wreck. Body parts littered the area around them. He took a deep breath and called the kid to come out.

The chaotic movement of people trying to get out mixed

with a cacophony of screams. Bile rose into his throat as the acrid smell of blood assaulted his nose.

"Keep your eyes shut, so the brightness out here doesn't hurt your eyes."

The kid mumbled something that amounted to something like "okay." Mark reached out his hand, and the kid grabbed it. Sharp objects were everywhere—twisted metal that turned into razor-sharp edges and dagger-like points. He led the kid through the rubble to the outside.

"You can open your eyes now, slowly."

The kid shielded his eyes with his right hand like a visor. The sun poked out on this cloudy day. "Thank you," the boy said, taking in the scene around him. "People…died today… didn't they?"

"Don't worry about that," Mark said, "because people die every day, so be grateful that you didn't."

The kid sat on the ground with his legs crossed. Mark finally let himself take in the scene. People milled about in a daze. Many sat on the embankment that led up to the street. Most were in shock and didn't know what to do.

Mark didn't want to be anywhere near the wreckage when the police and rescue started asking questions. He knew they'd somehow connect him to it. Irrational? Probably, but he believed it anyway.

Smoke from the wreckage rose up to the sky. He wandered away from the chaotic scene and train. When he felt he was at a safe distance, he turned back toward the chaos. The train cars had collided in a zigzag of metal rectangles, except for the one they just left and the one behind it. Half of the car was torn apart along the right side and roof.

Something powerful exploded—a pressure cooker bomb or something even more sinister.

It had only been eight years since the marathon bombing, and Boston had just gotten another. He shook his head at the destruction and bowed his head for the loss of life he knew, without a doubt, had been taken. Anger filled his head, and his body quivered, not out of shock but rage. Two of the cars were totally demolished—Debris had scattered in every direction for about 50 yards. It was even where he stood. He sighed and took a deep breath. He turned back to continue onward and almost knocked the kid down.

"What do we do now?" the boy asked in a pleading tone.

A child who needed to be told what to do next.

The boy was still in shock, and Mark wondered how long it would take him to recover. The boy wanted to know that everything would be all right. He could neither tell him things were good nor that nothing was okay about the situation.

"I don't know, kid, but I am not sticking around. You should go back down the hill and wait for the rescue to come and get checked out. The police and fire will be here any moment." Silence filled the air and lingered for some time. "Be sure to tell them what you saw. Go. Come on, get going."

"I don't want to stay," he said. The kid shook, and his voice had a little tremble." Can I go with you?"

"I don't know where I'm going."

"Then can you take me to my father's office?"

The kid stared at him with wide eyes that now started to tear. It tugged at his heart. Yeah, he was a criminal, but he still had morals, and though they were sometimes compromised, he wasn't all bad.

"Where's it at?"

"Downtown."

Mark couldn't tell the kid no. He just couldn't bring himself to do it. It wouldn't be the right thing to do. He should wait with the kid here, but his nerves wouldn't allow it. He needed to go now.

"Okay, let's go."

The kid smiled. The first one Mark saw on the kid's face all morning. They took one last look at the train wreckage and the billowing smoke that rose to the sky and blocked out the clouds.

They made it to the nearest street, and so far, they had been fortunate. If that train exploded underground, it would've been more tragic than it already was. Many more people would've lost their lives, but Mark wasn't sure how many had already died, but he was sure it was still a lot. He didn't need this right now, but he had no choice.

The kid, now filthy with his dirty, ripped, and tethered school uniform, had seen better days. Dirt and grime blemished the boy's innocent-looking face, and he imagined he didn't look much better.

They walked a couple of blocks to the nearest bus stop. People stared at them, giving them a wide berth as they passed by the onlookers. The acrid odor, which emanated from their clothing, suggested fire. However, the glances they received suggested something else altogether. Like they were diseased-ridden lepers. Vagrants. Look out of sorts, and the people in Boston will believe you're homeless and inflicted. The disgust plastered on their faces made him want to rip their faces off—*ignorant but educated people.*

A bus pulled over, and they boarded. Distracted by the entire situation, Mark didn't search their faces as he scanned the bus. They sat in the first available seat as the bus pulled off and drove down the bumpy city streets. They were no longer the smelliest. Two guys sitting across from them stunk up the bus like a distillery. He glanced at the boy, who was looking out the window. "How you holding up?"

"Okay, I guess," the boy said with a shrug.

"Me too. It's a scary thing that you just went through."

The boy turned and locked eyes with him. "Do you think people died back there?"

The question chilled the air, but he saw no reason to lie. "What do you think?"

"A lot had," the kid said, his voice starting to tremble. "Did you see the people at the other table? I think...they...were dead."

Mark hadn't noticed; he was too occupied with getting them out of there. He tried to remember, but he couldn't. "I didn't see them."

"The woman had blood covering her face...everything looked...I don't know...twisted. If–if you didn't pull me under the table—I would've been dead too."

The boy went quiet, so Mark glanced at him. Tears welled up in the kid's eyes. Just too much grief to bear for someone so young. Though Mark was a year or two younger when he saw his first dead body, he hoped the traumatic experience didn't scar the kid for life.

"It was the right thing to do, and believe me, kid, I don't ever do the right thing—it was about time."

The kid nodded but didn't reply. He just went back to staring out the window.

3

PARKER

JJ Parker had a rough life. He suffered severely, but today someone else would feel the same loss he had felt over the past several years. The loneliness. The grief mixed with rage. The people whom he had held accountable for all his pain would suffer. Today would be the day he finally got retribution for all his suffering.

It had taken years to plan this day just right. Though he had a particular target, society must also pay the price. The innocent bystanders need to partake in his suffering. They must learn the truth, and Parker was going to show them. Show them all! The American Dream was and always has been a farce built on lies. Live free...not in this country. The forefathers are rolling over in their graves at what this country and its people had become. Sheep...in the land of the free...on their way to the slaughter. Today, he'd prove it.

He stood at the end of the platform. *Good morning Boston.* Leaving the knapsack on the train was the easy part. Nobody seemed to notice. *Not a soul.* Parker was so sure, this being post-9/11 and post-marathon bombing, that someone would've noticed and alerted him he had forgotten his bag. *Nobody had.*

It needed to be where he left it to cause the maximum amount of damage…and the most casualties. The death of one in particular. They would never realize the whole thing was for one person. He was pleased that his target was aboard. Everything was going according to plan.

He fondled the fob he held in his hand. The fob had one button; he placed his finger over it. He waited as the train left the station. An impish grin upon his face. He sucked in air like death, sucking the life from a body. Once the last car disappeared into the tunnel, he turned and started counting as he headed for the exit.

One–two–three…he counted in his head at a steady pace. Time seemed to melt away as he reached the magic number and said aloud—twelve. Parker's eyes danced with anticipation as he pressed the button.

The explosion rocked the underground station—a powerful gust of air rushing past him. *Time to go.*

Parker wasn't done yet. Oh no. On the contrary, it was only the beginning. He had eleven bags placed randomly around the city. This would be a day Boston would never forget. He walked to the exit, climbed the stairs to the concourse, and exited the building.

He walked in the direction of the explosion. It took him two blocks before the smoke from the train wreckage came into view. A smile spread across his face, knowing the one person who needed to suffer—would.

A bus pulled over at the corner, where he stopped to admire the plume of smoke that rose into the air. He boarded—on his way to the next stop.

4

DETECTIVES

A thick tendril of smoke stretched into the darkening gray of the sky. Detective Franklin watched his partner approach. She was dressed in a bright spring-colored shirt that muted the misery around them. They observed the scene before them: medics attended the injured while uniform officers assisted survivors to ambulances and took statements.

The twisted wreckage of the train, with people wandering around confused and body bags beginning to stack up along the length of the train, made for a tough morning. Heart-wrenching. His stomach churned. How could another human being cause such terror?

His partner eyed him. "This is gonna be a long one, my friend," she said. "At least until the Feds come take it over."

"A long one, for sure," Franklin said. "They can have this

one. Hell, better them than us, but I guess we better get things started."

Detective Elizabeth Reynolds nodded rather grimly. He liked his partner because she held up more than her share and went the extra mile to get things done. It was tough during these times because it seemed like they were the few among the many. *The good guys*.

As if on cue, a uniformed officer approached. "Detective Franklin, I'm to bring you up to speed, and then the show is all yours."

"Wonderful," Franklin said with a shake of the head. Thank you, Sgt. Corin, I appreciate any information you can give us."

Sgt. Corin took the detectives on a tour of the disaster area. He pointed out a group of people they were approaching. "I think you might want to hear what these people have to say."

"Is it important, you think?" Reynolds asked.

"I'll let you decide what is or isn't important," Sgt. Corin said as they approached the four people. "These detectives are in charge. Can you tell them what you saw?"

"Sure, a big guy walked off—"

"He was mean-looking, too!" Another interjected.

"And he was with a white kid," yet another said.

"Whoa, hold up," Detective Franklin said. "One at a time." He pointed to the one in a red shirt. "You're first. You saw someone walk off?"

"Yeah, everyone waited for help to come, but this guy just took off—in a hurry."

"He was with a kid?" Reynolds added.

"I didn't see any kid."

"I did," a woman in a flower print blouse said.

Franklin motioned for her to continue, which was a big waste of time in the end. All the group saw was some guy with his kid. And yeah, it was strange for someone to leave after such a terrible disaster; however, it wasn't all that unusual. They had passed several dust-covered zombies on their way to the site. So he knew this lead would end up in the wastebasket. He glanced at Sgt. Corin, before thanking the nice people for their time and moved on.

"Sargent," he said as they walked away, "some of these buildings must have security cameras. Find me footage of this incident," he glanced at his watch. "From 30 minutes ago up until now. Right now. Got it?"

"Yes, sir," he said and walked off to do as he was ordered.

Franklin glanced over at his partner. "This is a nightmare."

"Tell me about it, so now what do we do?"

"For one, we need to find out what the hell happened and—"

"I think a bomb exploded."

"—catch the lunatic that did this."

"Now, I'm with you."

The two detectives took some more statements and helped where they could. Forty minutes later, Sgt. Corin came back with good news.

"I found three cameras that caught the entire thing," he said as he approached. "They're making copies as we speak. I left two officers behind to retrieve them. Also, I—"

The sergeant's radio squealed and then erupted with a flurry of commands. He put his ear to the speaker. "What the fuck," he said. "Looks like there's been another explosion."

"What?" Franklin said, shaking his head.

"Where?" Reynolds said.

The Sargeant told them it was only a few blocks away, but no one heard anything.

Franklin and Reynolds shook their heads. It was going to be a long day, for sure.

###

After a while, those who were hurt were triaged and either sent home or to a station house for further questioning. Most were sent home. Some of them still lingered. Detective Franklin made his way to the command station, a big box truck filled with high-tech equipment. The forensic team processed the train while he headed to the command center. On the way, he passed the pile of stacked body bags, which kept increasing in height.

At last count, there were a hundred. He knew there would be more. A lot more. He reached the command trailer and with a heavy heart, entered.

Franklin's partner greeted him as he entered.

"We've gone over the recordings that Sgt. Corin brought back. There's nothing out of the ordinary. Not a fucking thing."

"How about that guy," Franklin said. "The one with the kid."

"Yeah, we got footage of him," Reynolds said, " he wasn't the first one nor the last. Many people just left. Some have turned up in local hospitals. They've been busy with walk-ins all morning."

Franklin didn't know what to make of the situation. Nothing could make him understand how someone could carry out such an act. He just wanted to catch the son of a bitch. Too many people died…only a monster, a fucking monster, could have caused such a thing. The only thing he could hope for was to find the people responsible and punish them. The people of Boston were strong and would pull through as they had done in the past, but they needed closure first.

5

BUS RIDE

To add to the gloom, it started raining. As if the gods couldn't hold back their tears—the loss of life was too tragic. Mark found himself worried about the boy. It was a new feeling—concern mixed with empathy. Neither thing meant much to him in the past. He never cared about anyone besides himself. At least that's what he had been told time after time, but he knew it was true.

After a couple of stops, he started to relax the farther away they got. He could breathe, but had to get a grip on his emotions. His only priority at that moment was getting the kid to his father. *Nothing else mattered.* Irrational thoughts floated in his head that made him believe he'd get blamed for the attack because he's an ex-con. An easy out. He hated that label. He much preferred a formerly incarcerated person. But he knew the routine—once you go to prison, no one thinks you're human anymore.

Mark started scanning people's faces again—not trusting a soul. Not now. Never again.

The bus stopped to let people off. A guy rushed past. Though the man wore different attire—Mark was sure it was the guy from earlier. How did he miss him? Mark turned in his seat and scanned the back; he didn't see another backpack, but his internal alarm sounded loud and clear. *Get the fuck off the bus.*

Mark needed to follow the man but didn't know what to do with the kid. He could leave him on the bus. No, that wouldn't do. The kid wouldn't allow it.

He stood, grabbing the kid's hand. "Come on, let's go."

"This ain't our stop," the kid said in protest.

"I'll explain when we're off the bus," Mark said in a rushed fashion. "Come on, before we lose him."

"Lose who?"

"In a minute," Mark said as he dragged the kid off the bus. He scanned the sidewalk in both directions and then across the street. The man headed toward downtown. Mark walked in that direction with the kid trying hard to keep up."

"You're walking too fast. Who did you see?" the kid said, but he was unsure he wanted the answer.

"I think it's the same person I saw earlier on the train—before the explosion. But I'm not sure because he's wearing different clothes."

"Then maybe it isn't him."

They made it about 50 feet when a loud explosion rocked the ground, as a blast of hot air slammed into their backs, sending them face-first into the earth. They look back in horror. The bus they had just exited exploded and became engulfed in flames that licked the air above, and debris littered this street in a large radius.

He grabbed the boy and held him close, hiding his face so he couldn't see. He succumbed to his feelings. "Don't look," he warned the boy. I think we are best on foot, anyhow."

"It must've been him," the boy cried.

"It looks that way."

The sky opened up more, and rain poured down. The gods were again decrying their disappointment.

They made it a block when he realized he had forgotten about the man. He searched ahead, but in confusion, people rushed about. He had lost him.

"How far is your father's office from here?" He knew the area, but it no longer seemed familiar. Several years in prison could do that—things change. The world continues. It moves on with or without you.

"I don't know...I...never walked there from here. I've always taken the train to Downtown Crossing."

"Is it in the financial district?"

"It's near a triangular park with a parking garage underneath it."

"Well, if it's near there, we're about 15 minutes away by foot."

Mark found his pace quicken, but the kid kept up with no complaints. However, after a few blocks, he noticed the boy was getting tired, so he slowed down. They walked for ten minutes in complete silence—the rain soaking their clothes. Neither of them seemed to notice.

The kid broke the silence.

"Hey–um–I'm...cold," he said. "And you know, I don't even know your name. What is it?"

"It's Mark. What's yours?"

"Brian," he said, then sucked his teeth. "How come you're not scared?"

"Believe me, Brian, I am. Very much so. But right now, the most important thing I need to do is get you to your dad's work."

"Oh...what about that man?" he said with a stutter—an obvious chill.

Mark was sure the cold rain didn't cause it.

"When the bus exploded and threw us to the ground, I lost sight of the guy."

The kid seemed satisfied with the answer and went back to being quiet. The rain let up. *Don't think too hard, Lil man*, he thought. He spotted a vending cart selling sausages and pretzels under a canopy. The vendor appeared to be closing up for the day—the rain choosing for him. Mark was suddenly thirsty. His throat was dry.

"Hey, Brian, want something?" He said as he stopped at the cart.

Brian eyed the pretzels spinning on the heated rack.

"Let me get a raspberry iced tea and two pretzels," Mark said, flashing a fake smile at the kid. "Now, what do you want?"

Despite all he'd been through, Brian cracked a smile. Albeit briefly due to guilt.

Mark handed the vendor a $20 bill, and the man quickly gave him his change. The unlikely pair walked on. They were almost there.

Mark took a more circuitous route. Better safe than dead. The sky opened with a flash and a roar—rain pouring down on them again. They stopped under an overhang of a building to eat their food. He could see Boylston Street Station from where they stood. Mark felt safe because the downpour obscured all lines of sight. Once the kid finished, they headed underground into the subway station.

The kid started talking about everything and anything. He told Mark he liked to draw and didn't have many friends. The kid was a waterfall of information. Mark recognized that he was talking so he wouldn't think about what had happened. He preferred this over the kid being quiet. He wasn't sure what he had done. If anything, whatever caused it, he was grateful. Now, if only he could distract himself from his own thoughts.

Something nagged at his consciousness. But it wouldn't–couldn't–push through. He glanced around, surveying the area as they walked down the steps into the train station. He had to keep the kid safe. The only thing he knew with certainty—was he'd do whatever it took.

Mark searched everybody's face as they passed, even of those he saw across the tracks. So far, things look good. He listened to Brian. Nodded and answered his every question while he kept watching. With his nerves rattled, his senses clicked on to full alert, telling him that danger lurked in the shadows around him.

The bomber's face nagged him. He tried to remember how he knew the man and what he could've done to cause someone to go to such lengths to kill him. So many innocent people. His inner voice kept breaking through his thoughts: not what you had done. *Remember.* Remember what? He screamed at himself. What was there to remember? *Not what,* that voice back again, *but who?* Who?

The train pulled into the station, screeching to a halt. The boy grabbed onto his arm—and stiffened as he gripped it tight. They boarded, taking up a position where Mark could see everyone on board. He resumed scanning faces.

6

HOW CAN THIS BE

The man walked to the back of the bus and sat on the left side next to a window, with his back against the wall. He felt the heat of the engine emanating through the back of the seat. With a Bluetooth earpiece in place, he glanced down at the iPhone in his hand. In time to see a—BREAKING NEWS—update, streaming live footage of the train bombing.

Although the official cause hadn't been made, several new stations already began calling it a terror attack. So dramatic. Nevertheless, Parker liked it. He liked it very much. The raw footage showed complete devastation. The death total rose to 102 and counting. He smiled to himself. Most of the dead were in the immediate area of the blast. The train car where the bomb was located meant nobody in that car survived.

The screen filled with images of the scene—dozens of dirty, disheveled people, most likely passengers, milled about in total disbelief. Some hung their heads down as they shuffled about. The camera panned through a crowd of the still living. Parker was pleased…he didn't…see him. Not in any of the footage, and that was a good sign. Perfect. The first part of the plan was complete. He changed clothes right there in the back of the bus before gazing out the window for a moment and reveling in his accomplishment. He had waited many, many years for this day to come and was finally here. *They will pay.*

He closed the news app—the program disappearing from view. An app icon that glowed on the screen caught his attention. That shouldn't be working, should it? Puzzled, he blinked and clicked on the icon to open the program—a GPS tracking app. A blue dot moved along the screen. How can that be?

He enlarged the map to get a better view to determine where the dot was located. The device was hidden in a piece of clothing, so it shouldn't be working. It had cost Parker a considerable sum to have it made and switched out. Maybe someone stole it, but that didn't make any sense. The bus slowed to a stop to pick up passages—just as the dot enlarged—Parker's eyes went wide. He glanced out the window and couldn't believe his eyes. Fuck, he's alive. And he immediately knew why. He underestimated the situation. Fate had intervened, but luck had brought them right to him. He glanced at the backpack in between his legs on the floor. The explosive devices within the bag were meant for a different destination; however, killing Mark Toren and the little brat with him had to be done first. So help him, it would.

Mark and the kid boarded the bus and took a seat on the same side he was seated. Parker could see the back of Mark's head several rows ahead as he opened the knapsack and removed several silver disks and a cellphone. Parker turned on the cellphone, pressed several buttons, and dropped it back into the bag. He then zipped it back up and pushed the bag under the empty seat in front of him. He pressed the call strip to signal the bus to stop.

The bus slowed as it pulled over. Parker stood, removed one of the disks, and pressed the button on its face, programming it to be recognized with the ones inside the knapsack. He walked to the front of the bus and stopped to "tie his shoe" as he slid the disk under the seat behind Mark and the boy. After the bus pulled over, he stood and stumbled off. Revenge would be his. Mark wouldn't ruin his plans a second time. Oh, no…not…a second time. *Death will be his prize*, he thought, as he exited the bus and fled up the street.

When he was a safe distance away, he stopped, removed his iPhone, and placed a call to the phone in the knapsack, which forwarded the call to a number that would be picked up automatically—triggering several disks to ignite when the call was answered. A robotic voice said activated. He closed the phone. Before he could turn back in the direction, the bus exploded. Traffic stopped as people ran in all directions. Someone screamed.

The bus was blown in half, completely destroyed. Nobody could have survived such a blast. Thick smoke blocked his vision. The bus was engulfed in flames. He felt relieved at seeing the sight of the burning bus and elated by the horror of those watching on. People were screaming as they ran past him. He took in the horrific scene and decided it would be best if he weren't around—sirens pierced the air.

You'll be busy today, he thought as he ducked down an alley, which he knew would bring him close to his next target. Though the bus wasn't part of the plan, it would still get the message across. No one's safe. America isn't safe. Loved ones die…and no one cares. But they will now. At least for a little while. The rest must pay for what they have done. Or didn't do, which was more to the point, but they all will pay today.

7

PARK STATION

Mark couldn't shake the feeling—he knew the man, but from where? He searched the faces of the people waiting on the platform as they pulled into the next station and of those who boarded the subway car as he racked his brain for the answer. He knew the answer was always—obvious— right there in front of you. So because of its subtlety. There had to be something. What? What was he missing? The doors to the car closed, and the train moved on to the next stop—Park station.

Their stop.

The commuter train, bus, and him being in both places had to be coincidental. At least, that's what he kept telling himself. Just a coincidence. Regardless of what he really believed. He glanced over at the kid. Brian, who continued to look out the window, stopped, turned, and met his gaze.

"Do you think he's gonna…do it…again?"

The boy's voice was shaky. Fearful.

Mark decided there was no reason to lie to the kid. The boy was intelligent and probably was only looking for confirmation of what he already knew. "Unfortunately, yes. I believe he will."

"That's what I thought. Thanks."

"For what?"

"Most adults would lie to protect a kid…thinking…we can't handle it, but—"

"They're the ones that really can't," Mark finished the line.

Brian smiled. "Well, if that's true…that he'll do it again… we shouldn't be taking public transportation."

Mark cracked a smile. Intelligent indeed. "No, we probably shouldn't," Mark said in a solemn but hopeful tone. "But we're coming into our stop now."

"That's good—"

Mark glanced back at the kid.

"—I didn't want to tell you…but…I'm scared."

"I know," he said, touching the kid's chin, "and I'll get you to your dad's office—in one piece. He wanted to finish it with an "I promise," but he knew nobody could promise such a thing. Not when a madman was blowing up everything in sight. According to the man who sat next to them, 180 people had already been killed. Mark knew he and the boy were lucky to be alive.

The train came to a stop. The doors opened. Brian stood and started to walk toward them—Mark pulled him back. "Not yet. Wait for some people to leave first, okay?"

Brian nodded but said: "Why? Do you think he's out there?"

"I don't know. He could be," Mark said, "but it's probably just my overactive imagination. Come on, let's go."

Brian nodded again, understanding perfectly, and followed him off the train.

Mark scanned the concourse, which was jampacked with humanity. However, most were not headed for another train. Instead, they headed toward the exit. No longer feeling safe, Mark assumed, and he didn't blame them, but he was surprised that people weren't freaking out.

Boston Strong.

The atmosphere in the station was more of caution than panic. Bostonian's had experienced a bombing before, and today they showed what Boston Strong meant.

Along with the moving mass of bodies, they headed for the stairs. The way out. Some people entered the station while others switched trains, but they were definitely in the minority. Still, no panic, despite many people's faces showing fear.

They slowly moved away from their car and toward the exit. The mass of humanity swallowed them up. They were in the midst of the crowd—and that's when he caught sight of the man. *Shit!*

The kid immediately sensed something was wrong and grabbed hold of Mark's hand, then tugged.

Brian also saw the man.

Mark squatted down and met Brian's gaze and saw terror glaze over the sparkle in Brian's eyes. "He's in control, but we can't give up, okay. We need to get out of here."

Mark glanced back toward the top of the stairs, where the man stood on the platform. Halfway from the exit. The man locked eyes with Mark…and smiled. A familiar, all-knowing smile. One he'd seen before, but where he couldn't recall. The man stuffed one hand into his left coat pocket, still smiling as he nodded, then turned to walk up the stairs. Shit, shit, shit!

Mark glanced around, looking for—he tugged Brian along through the crowd headed for a brick structure. A concession stand made out of the same bricks as the station. Another two feet and they would be safe—

Not one, but several explosions erupted around them, sending debris and people into the air, including Mark and the kid. Mark landed heavily on his chest while Brian somersaulted forward and landed on his butt. Then another explosion. Mark closed his eyes. They choked back the thick smoke that filled the concourse.

The entire event took less than thirty seconds, but the explosion alone felt like an eternity to Mark. Reality slowed down as everything appeared to be in slow motion.

Mark waited…until…he counted to sixty. No more explosions. After a deep breath, he scrambled to Brian and clutched him in his arms. A bearhug shield. He could feel Brian's heart slamming in his chest. "Are you okay?"

"Yeah, I think so," Brian said, "but my ears are ringing bad."

"Mine too," Mark said, getting to his feet as he helped Brian up. "Come on, let's go!"

The concourse was still filled with rich gray smoke. Flames licked the ceiling in several places. The stench of burning plastic and flesh permeated the air. People scrambled for the exits. Many more littered the floor—some groaning in pain while others' ear-piercing screams haunted his soul. Many were dead.

"Brian, concentrate on the exit, all right?"

"Why…um oh…they…D–dead—"

"Yes, concentrate on the exit. Look at the foggy gray light at the top of the stairs. You see it? That's safety," Mark said as they climbed over the dead and up the slick, bloodstained stairs toward the light and the safety beyond.

Brian continued to talk. "I like rock climbing…but don't think anywhere is safe. Not anymore. Anyhow. Did you know my favorite color is blue?"

Mark didn't reply; he knew Brian was distracting himself by talking. Just like he had done earlier after the bus exploded. Regardless, he had to agree: no place was safe anymore. Mark felt the same way. *Deeply.* They made it to the middle landing, where the man stood moments earlier.

"Just a little farther," he urged. "Come on. We can do this."

People scurried around them, heading toward the safety of the surface ahead. The stairs had become even slicker due to the sprinkler system being activated. It was slow going, for sure. People took a few steps and slid back to where they had begun. Mark, like Brian, climbed slightly ahead of him. But he stayed right behind him, holding onto one of Brian's belt loops. Moments later, they were free and being directed by emergency workers toward a makeshift triage. Mark declined to be checked, stating they were fine, and if any problems developed later, they'd go to the emergency room.

They wandered into the Common and sat down on a park bench. "Listen, your dad is right around—" he cut himself off. "Fuck. *Why?*"

Brian followed his line of sight and saw the man. "Is that him?"

The man's pace slowed as he glanced over his shoulder before turning left down a side street.

"I believe so."

"Now what?" Brian asked with a tremor in his voice.

"We follow him."

"I was afraid you were gonna say that."

8

TAKE THAT

Parker smiled. He only had a block to go to his next destination. The office building loomed overhead. Earlier in the day, he placed several explosive devices around town. Set to be used as a distraction so that he could hit his real targets. The devices were in buses, trash barrels, subway stations, and cars, and one was even stuffed in between the back seat of a cab. Extensive preparation went into the day's events.

Mark was severely fucking things up on him. At least that asshole was now dead, so he hoped. Parker wondered why Mark was with the kid. Who was Mark to the brat? Nevertheless, he wanted him—both of them—dead. Deciding not to look a gift horse in the mouth, he removed his cellphone and clicked on the glowing icon that told him it was still activated. Though the GPS should have been destroyed in such a—wait, he wasn't surprised to see the dot moving.

However, what did surprise him was that the dot was moving away from the scene. It aggravated him to no end. He stared at the dot, and it winked out—disappearing from existence. Maybe his suspicion was unwarranted…but he knew better. As to answer his question, the blue dot blinked back on. What the hell? No! He understood what happened; they must be below in the subway. Dammit, they had to be first. He had to be first—must follow the plan. He stopped and turned left. In a full run, he ran toward Park Station, only a few city blocks away.

Parker fumed. He stopped running, flagged down a cab, and jumped into the back, not wanting to waste any more time than he had to. "Park station, and make a quick."

The cabbie glared at him through the rearview mirror.

Parker removed a $100 bill from his wallet and stuffed it into the plexiglass divider pay box. The cabbie turned to see what his fair put in the box and smiled. "Okay, my friend, I'll get you there in two seconds." He shouted through the plexiglass before stepping on the gas.

Three hundred seconds later, the cabbie dropped Parker off at Park Street station. He wasn't sure how Mark kept them out of harm's way, but he had done just that so far. The sheer thought of him being still alive pissed him off.

The rain stopped. Though the clouds overhead were dark and ominous, Parker trekked across the wet concrete to the subway's entrance. He ran down the stairs as he removed his phone and paid to get in. Once through the turnstile, Parker fumbled with his phone. The blue dot stopped, and as he watched, it started moving toward him. They were at the stop before this one and headed right to him. A mischievous grin appeared on his stoic face. He waited a few minutes and returned the way he'd come. When he reached the middle landing, he heard a train enter the station, so he stopped to check the dot, which proclaimed them to be right where he was. They're here.

He was so happy that he chose the station as part of his planned distraction, but this purpose was much nobler. When the train came to a stop, the doors opened, and a rush of people exited, heading straight for the exit toward him. The news had spread. His plan was working. The lambs were getting the message—you're not safe. Nowhere and never have been. He was elated. But where were Mark and the kid? He checked the screen on the phone one more time. The dot had moved. Where were they? He waited for everyone to exit the train.

People push past him.

On the landing, he waited and watched until the last person debarked. He saw more movement as two people, an adult, and a child, exited the train. But before he could smile, he saw it wasn't them. Two more riders left by the front doors of the trolley. He smiled this time because it was them. They were directly in his line of sight. What made it even better was the mass of humanity had swallowed them up into their ranks. No place to run. End of the line for Mark and the brat. He stayed focused on Mark, and as if sensing Parker's gaze, he looked directly at him, and they locked eyes. Parker reached into his pocket and smiled. His hand wrapped around another cellphone and he pressed send. He removed his hand from his pocket, waved good-bye to Mark, and turned before running back up the stairs, pushing his way through the crowd.

Parker barely made it out of the exit when the first succession of explosions rumbled somewhere behind him.

9

ENOUGH IS ENOUGH

Hundreds of people milled about, watching the scene unfold like a movie shoot. Police roped off the area around the entrance and exit. Mark glanced around the park. Those around him and Brian, who were also in the explosion, sought refuge in the Common. The Boston Common. Benches and grassy spaces were filled with dirty people who looked like the weight of the world had just crushed them.

Misty gray cloud of smoke hung low over the park.

Mark glanced down at the boy. "You can stay in the park, or we can ask the police officers to take you to your dad?"

Brian shook his head violently. "No! I wanna stay with you." The emphatic tone made him appear younger than twelve.

Mark wasn't sure what to do—and truth be told, he didn't want to leave the boy alone. He especially didn't want to trust some cop, or anyone else, for that matter. "Are you sure?"

Brian nodded.

"All right, let's go," he said as they left the Common and crossed Tremont Street.

Mark could still see the man walking down the side street in a hurry. There was a bus stop on that street, and he wondered if he was going for it. A bus turned the corner and pulled over. He was sure the man would get on the bus, but he walked straight past, heading toward Macy's.

He figured the man was headed to Downtown Crossing, which was in the direction he went. If he turned left at the end of the street, it would be Downtown Crossing, but if he turned right, he would be headed toward Chinatown. Though the street didn't continue onward, he could cut through Macy's and come out on the other side at the corner of summer and whatever the other street was named.

He wondered where the man was headed. Was he watching the exits for them? Had he seen them? He hoped it wasn't a setup. The man just casually walked along as if he had no care in the world. The man's step was almost giddy. He started to believe it wasn't a trap. The side street was crowded with people, some shopping or waiting for the bus—and others with soot-stained clothes, like their own, roamed about like zombies.

Mark even thought about buying some new clothes, an irrational thought but one he had. Along with sudden chest pain, he pushed the thoughts and feelings aside and continued onward. They followed the man, who now appeared to be using his cellphone—seeing the man with the phone made Mark cringe. It could be what he used to activate the bombs.

The man turned left without warning, went up the street, and took a sharp right into the Corner Mall. The mall now only held a handful of shops but was the food court for the downtown shopping area. Maybe they'll be getting something to eat after all.

They quickened their pace and followed him into the mall. The food court was busy. Mark scanned the dining area along with each takeout line. *Nothing.* They began to leave the food court. Maybe the man was just cutting through and headed for the Washington Street exit, which didn't make sense, seeing a just left Washington Street. They were about the pass Dunkin' Donuts when Brian tugged on Mark's shirt. He turned to see what the kid wanted. Brian nodded back to the dining area. At first, Mark didn't say anything.

"The Chinese place," Brian said in a small voice.

In the line in front of the Chinese food stall, they saw the man. Since they were standing in front of Dunkin' Donuts, they stepped into line and placed an order. Once they received their food, they found a table in the dining area before the man could pick up his order. Brian ate a cinnamon twist donut and drank hot chocolate, as Mark did the same.

Brian started talking. Doing that, *I'm nervous, so I'll talk about random things* again. To everyone else, he just appeared to be a normal kid, albeit dirty and tattered. Not one with PTSD symptoms. Mark welcomed the normality of it. Luckily, he watched the man take his order to a seat where Mark could watch him clearly. As Mark kept his eye on him, he talked to Brian.

Brian rambled on about liking to draw. Mark made a pretense of being really interested. The man picked up his phone without looking at it, put it to his ear, and started talking. Being this close, Mark got a great look at him: a black male of above-average height and large build with a head of reddish-brown hair.

The man seemed to be in his midtwenties, possibly in his early thirties, but he wasn't positive. He was never good at judging someone's age. Mark knew one thing for sure; he definitely knew the man, except the who and the where were elusive. Something hindered the connection. The man's face was somehow off. Whatever he was missing—it was key to this mess.

Mark brought his cup up to his mouth. Empty. Surprised, he looked down and realized he had finished his drink and donut. He crumpled up the wrapper and stuffed it into the Dunkin' Donuts bag. Brian, who had just finished, handed Mark his trash. He took the garbage from Brian as he watched the man who was no longer talking on his phone. Instead, he held it sideways and viewed the screen. Probably a newsfeed.

The man suddenly looked around…got up, headed out the food court, and straight to the Washington Street exit. Mark wondered why he was in such a hurry. Mark grabbed their trash, tossed it in the nearest receptacle, and followed him.

The sun was trying to peek out from behind the gray sky. Mark checked both directions—up and down Washington Street. The pedestrian-only portion of the street was busy with people, but he was nowhere in sight. *Damn, he moved fast.* Mark turned back and motioned to Brian, who stood inside, just beyond the glass door, to come on. They headed up Washington Street.

"You know where you are, right?"

"Yeah…I think so," Brian stammered. "Chipotle is up that way, isn't it?"

"It is."

"Then my dad's office is that way," Brian said, pointing at a 45° angle through the buildings on the right side of the street.

"Do you remember the street or the building's name?"

"Nah, I'll try to remember, but I know the way."

"That's even better. Lead the way, Lil man," Mark said as they continued up Washington Street. They walked in silence. Brian held onto his hand. Mark had many questions: Had the man spotted them? Where did he go? What the fuck was really going on? He had no answers. But he was more certain than ever that he was the reason and just didn't know why.

He glanced down at Brian as they crossed a small side street approaching the jeweler's building. He could see the green flag flapping in the wind. Mark wondered if Kal was still a jeweler in the building to the left. Brian tugged his hand when they were a few feet from the building's entrance. Brian wandered across to the other side. Mark complied. They then took the next right just after the CVS.

As They Walked Down Milk St., Mark continued to think about the man. There was something about him that nagged him to no end. It reached a remote part of Mark's subconscious brain, but whatever the thought had been, it faded fast, like his short-term memory. He pushed it aside. The only thing he could truly rely on, at the moment, were facts. Today he was released. Fact. He recognized the man. Fact. Three separate bombings. Fact. He had to make a decision that needed to be made fast.

He couldn't keep putting Brian's life in danger. The kid wanted to stay with him—to be safe—but Mark felt it was him who put Brian in harm's way. He glanced around. Few people were on their side of the street. Only those in business suits. A good sign, so he believed. But he felt as though he was being watched—and that was not such a good feeling.

"Hold up, Brian," he said as they stopped in front of where the old Boston Stock Exchange had been. Now a 30-story tower.

Brian stared at Mark with his penetrating bluish-green eyes. He swallowed hard. "You...you want me to go to my dad's... by myself," he said, more as a statement than a question.

Perceptive kid, Mark thought. "Brian, I think this man is out to get me, and apparently, he doesn't care who he kills in the process." Brian grabbed his hand. Tears welled up in his eyes, "so I need to make him follow me to a place where he can't harm any more people."

"But–you–you...could die."

"That's possible," he said, "but believe me...I'm gonna try like hell...not to."

Brian wiped his face. They started walking again. "My dad's office is only a few more blocks. It's not that far."

"I think he saw us back there and could be—possibly— watching us right now." Brian looked around. "So, I can't keep putting you in danger, do you understand?"

Brian just nodded. His eyes filled up with tears, ready for another round. They stopped at the next corner. Brian had to go straight, and Mark had to go left. He knew there was a bus and the train stop just past Faneuil Hall. Mark figured that public transportation service would shut down soon if it hadn't already. Sirens could still be heard. Mark knew there was also a taxi stand in that direction, and he could take one if that's what was needed. He'd do anything for Brian right now, which is what he had to do. He glanced to the left, his destination, then back to Brian.

"Go on," he urged. "You'll be safe, I promise." He placed his hands on Brian's shoulders. "You're a smart kid, and I am proud to have met you."

"Me too," Brian said, then he hugged Mark tightly, not wanting to let go and burying his face in Mark's chest. After a moment, Mark told him it was time to go. Brian reluctantly pulled himself away, wanting to cry, but he fought it back. He looked up, meeting Mark's eyes. "I'll see you again, right?"

"I don't know what to tell you. I don't know," Mark said with the slightest amount of regret. "But—"

"When it's over."

"When it's over," Mark answered.

Brian swallowed hard, took a deep breath as he pulled away, and walked onward to his father's office building. The dam of tears letting go.

Mark just hoped the kid would be all right. He was confident Brian understood why he couldn't take him any farther. He just hoped he could draw this lunatic away from the kid and other people. He had to get him as far away from the city as possible. And Mark had a plan. He watched Brian cross the street to the other side and continue onward, wiping his face repeatedly as he did.

Mark glanced around, still having that 'someone's watching me' feeling, and thought, *that's right, buddy, I'm right here—come on and get me.*

He walked toward the taxi stand—

The trash receptacle he had just left exploded on the corner. Mark turned as the blast sent him down to the ground. *Fuck.* He heard another explosion—it came from Brian's direction. He was suddenly on his feet with agility he didn't know he had and ran toward the other explosion—toward Brian. The other exploded trash receptacle was halfway up the street. Smoke filled the air. Mark held his breath, and if Brian hadn't made it or was even hurt, he wouldn't be able to forgive himself. Had he made a mistake in his decision to split up?

If he did…

He could and would make this lunatic pay with his life. Then from within the smoke emerged a small figure—the apparition materialized into Brian. Thank God. Relief filled his body. Brian saw him and started running, and so did Mark. He put out his arms, and Brian jumped into them. He cared for this kid. They had a bond. One Mark couldn't quite comprehend but knew the day's tragic events caused it. They crossed the street when they were a couple of blocks away. First, he looked around, seeing nothing that could explode. Mark hadn't even remembered walking.

"All right, Lil man, plans have changed. Let's go."

They walked in the direction Brian needed to go. Their pace quickened with every urgent step, and at the next corner, they turned right.

"How you holding up, kid? You, okay?"

"I'm good. Just get me to my dad's"

"I will. No matter W—"

Brian looked up.

"*Fuck,*" Mark said under his breath…. A figure stood approximately 15 feet away, but there was no mistaking the man. He stood confidently, eyes locked on them, with his cellphone in his hand—and a knowing smile on his face.

Turning back, they ran toward the street they had just come to. A lonely bicycle courier peddled toward them. They quicken their pace. Mark picked up Brian—knowing he could run faster, even with the extra weight. Brian hung on tightly for his life. Mark glanced back. The man hadn't moved. Not an inch. That knowing smile remained plastered on his face. Mark whipped his head around as the bike messenger approached them. There were no cars on the street. The street was too narrow, and no parking was allowed. He watched the messenger as he started to pass them—then he ran to the nearest doorway. One that was inset. He put Brian down—just as the bike messenger exploded into a spray of red.

The explosion sent Mark crashing into the stone stairs.

He was in pain—his thigh was on fire. He crawled up the stairs to the small landing, where Brian cowered in the corner, screaming. No kid should have to scream like that. The terrified look on his face made Mark ask if he was okay. "I'm okay," Brian said as Mark propped himself up against the wall next to Brian and checked his leg.

Something from the explosion stuck in his leg. He grabbed at the spot and found a sliver of debris that Mark believed to be bone—some part of the bike messenger. The thought sent a shudder of repulsion up his spine as bile rose in his throat. Tears welled up from the pain. Though it'd probably be wiser to leave it in, Mark knew he wouldn't make it far doing so, so he yanked it out—with a howl of pain. He tossed the foreign splinter to the ground and peeked around the corner—nobody in sight. However, they could hear sirens in the distance getting louder. Sirens were a mainstay of this day.

"Come on, Brian, we need to get the fuck outta here." And with that, they took off, moving as fast as possible, knowing the man could be lurking around the next corner.

10

DAMN COCKROACHES

The cordoned-off area quickly filled up with survivors and, of course, the dead. Parker watched from beyond the yellow police tape. Across the street, actually. Far enough away to just be another rubbernecker, one whose curiosity made them stop to see what was going on and nothing more. Intently, he watched those who were ambulatory exit the station. When the last of the stragglers came out, about 15 minutes had passed, he decided they were probably among the dead. The body bags started to pile up, and it made him smile. *This is what they get because no one will tell them the truth—nobody is safe.*

Courts protect the monsters among us. They'll get it now.

To be safe, he *scanned* the area, including the park, but saw no one resembling Mark or the kid. Assuming they hadn't got split up in the melee. He wasn't looking for them separately, so that could have been what happened. But he knew that if Mark hadn't left the kid by now, he wasn't going to. Though he could hope, it would certainly make things easier. He scanned the triage area once more before moving on.

He checked his watch. It was just after 11 AM. His next target would have to wait because this situation complicated things just a little. He needed to kill at least 20 minutes or so for the guard he knew to come back on duty. His stomach growled. He remembered to eat breakfast, but all this extra running around had burned those calories. His body told him it was time to eat lunch. So he headed to the Corner Mall's food court. The Chinese place there served food he'd be willing to eat.

When he turned down the side street leading to Downtown Crossing and his destination, he got this overwhelming sense of being watched—he turned back, searching for the faces of the people behind him. Nothing. Just his overactive imagination. He kept walking, and he felt light in his step. Nothing could ruin the high—so good—feeling he felt. Seconds later, he turned left onto Winter Street, in case someone was following, and then down the short alley into the Corner Mall Food Court. The minute the cold air hit him, mother nature called, so he ran downstairs to the restroom.

After taking care of his business, he went upstairs and got in line at the Chinese food place. He ordered food, picked it up, and took it to the nearest empty table. He tore into the chicken broccoli stir-fry. As he ate, his cellphone buzzed in his pocket. He removed the phone and answered it without ever seeing who it was. If he had, he would've let it go straight to voicemail.

"Hello?"

"It's me," the caller said. "Where are you? Have you seen the TV?"

"Yes, I know. What's up? Look, was there something you needed, because if it was just the news coverage, then obviously, I know what's going on, so is there anything else?"

Silence on the other end.

Parker shook his head. "I said don't call unless it's important." He said before hanging up the phone before the caller could reply.

The kid was good at running errands, but he had absolutely no brain. Dumb as an ox. Oh well, good help was hard to find these days. Besides, the kid will do his part when the time comes—and soon. He checked his iPhone screen for the time. He had a few moments before he had to go. Curiously, the GPS icon glowed, so he opened the app to see if it was working yet.

It took a moment for the program to fully open, but when it did—his jaw dropped. Immediately, he looked around. How can this be? He glanced back at the screen. On the screen was a glowing blue dot, and the location printed beside it was his own. They were somewhere inside the building. They could be upstairs, he thought. Then he decided against it and searched the food court once more—

Bingo.

They were less than 20 feet away. Somehow, the game changed. Mark was now following him. And with the boy in tow. That didn't seem like Mark. No, not at all. Where are you going? Parker smiled, thinking he knew. At least, he hoped.

He picked up his tray and tossed out his garbage before he bolted for the Washington Street exit. Of course, he clenched his phone in his hand, with the GPS program open.

"Come on, Mark, Chase me," he muttered to himself aloud, then thought, you'll find the table has been turned once again. This is my game you're playing, and I'll make sure you play by my rules. My rules, buddy. Then he laughed, a man-acle laugh, as he crossed the street and disappeared down a side street. He made it two blocks, checking the GPS as he went. He stopped as he watched the blue dot quickly move up Washington Street. "That's right, come to me."

This day wasn't going according to plan, notat all, but Parker had to admit that the challenges Mark had brought to the table at least made it exciting. Maybe even interest-ing. Fool me once, shame on you; fool me twice, shame on me—and that's not gonna happen. He almost jumped for joy when they turned down Milk Street because he was a block away on the same street. He watched from the shadow of the nearest doorway and waited for Mark and the kid. According to the dot's position, he should see them any second—and he did. When they stopped at the corner next to a trash recep-tacle, he laughed—and thanked God. Another part of his distraction plan included several explosive devices planted inside an array of trash bins, and that was one of them.

The other was halfway up the block on the same side. But if they turn down Congress Street, all would be lost. There were no devices that way. He picked up the throwaway cell-phone and scrolled through the list of names, which were coded for locations, then pressed the call button. It rang once and hung up. He looked at the screen. Zero bars. Shit, maybe it's the concrete surrounding him, he thought as he walked down the steps to the sidewalk. Still nothing. He didn't want to use the iPhone, but he had no choice but to dial the number. He got as far as the sixth digit when he noticed the kid, and Mark seemed to be having it out.

Were they going to split up?

Of course they were. Parker quickly punched in the rest of the numbers and hit send. But it was too late; they had already started to walk away, with Mark going down the side street and the kid continuing toward him. Parker smiled anyway. At least he'd get to kill the kid. Parker's phone sang a particular melody. He answered and quickly hung up the call and called a different number.

The trashcan exploded, showering debris down upon the street. People scattered as cars stopped—one even crashed into the back of the one in front of it. Chaos. Just what he liked. The kid stopped, unsure if he should go back, though he took several more steps. He missed Mark, but he would not miss the kid. He pressed send, and a moment later, the closer trashcan exploded. More people scattered. Cars honked. Smoke obscured his view, but he heard screams and the sound of glass tinkling, followed by the crunch of metal.

The scene was pleasantly chaotic. A sight to see, Parker was sure. The smoke dissipated, at least enough, and in time for him to see the kid jump into Mark's arms—and cross over to the side of the street. Fuck. Parker left the safety of the shadow with haste to get away from Mark and the boy. He walked hurriedly to the next street and turned right. The street was narrow. No cars. It was perfect because his next stop was only a block away. He could see the top of the building as he turned down the street.

The throwaway also had a GPS tracking program—and he used this program to track the devices he had planted to cause utter panic. They seem to be doing just that. Out of the eleven dots that were there at the beginning of the day, only four remained. Plus, the ones in his pockets. The one he was checking on made him smile. He was smiling a lot this day, which was unusual. He hadn't smiled in years.

Mark and the kid turned down the street and walked several yards before Mark noticed him, and they stopped dead. Parker smiled impishly and slightly nodded to them, though he doubted they saw it.

A bike messenger turned onto the street. Mark and the kid ran to the nearest doorway. But they weren't going to make it. The messenger approached them as Parker pressed send. He always wanted to see one of those fuckers' blowup—and a second later, he got his wish as the messenger disappeared into a cloud of blood, guts, and entrails. *Yuck.*

The blast knocked Mark to the ground. He smiled as Mark dragged himself to the stoop. The kid was already hiding. A moment later, he heard a howl of pain.

Without warning, they burst from the stoop in a half-jog–run. Parker was sure he knew where they were headed, but they ran back the way they had come, away from that direction. He headed toward there and let them tire themselves out, thinking he could be around the next corner. He had to admit this was much more fun than his original plan. A lot more. He followed them with the GPS, and when they got close, he'd get them. Both.

Still, he thought, *fucking cockroaches.*

11

NEWS

Mark scanned the area after they stopped running, which was closer to a trot. Both of them were winded and panting. He couldn't believe they had run so far, in the wrong direction—almost back to where they started. Fear was no friend. They stopped in front of a small glass structure that occupied the end of a small alley. The coffeehouse newsstand catered to the foot traffic of the local businesspeople in the area.

The television in the window caught Mark's attention. It was there to grab the attention of passersby, and it did exactly that.

Breaking News flashed on the screen and chronicled the morning's horrific events. It, however, wasn't surprising at all. He expected the news channels to be stuck on the incident all day and for weeks to come. Like they did with the marathon bombing and 9/11.

What surprised Mark was the picture of a group of people on the television. Survivors. The camera focused on one of them—the man. Mark stopped and pulled Brian to the television, where a small, somber crowd had gathered.

Those around him and Brian were transfixed, their gaze never leaving the television. Their facial expressions displayed an array of mixed emotions: horror, disgust, anguish, and of course, disbelief. Mark was sure empathy was mixed in there somewhere as well.

Before Mark made it close enough to the TV, the picture switched to a scene at Park Station, then to where the bike messenger got killed, and then back to the station and a news anchor. Mark asked a woman, who was standing next to him, what they said about the man.

"Nothing. Nothing at all. They were just survivors of that explosion," she said flatly, without emotion. "This world is going crazy. It's the end of days, I tell you. Heaven, help us?" she said, finally taking in Mark and the boy. A look of surprised understanding contorted her face. "Oh, I'm sorry," she said, handing Mark a religious tract. "May God bless you."

Mark, who wasn't particularly religious, glanced down at himself in the boy, then tousled Brian's hair. "I believe he already has, don't you?"

The woman smiled wanly before moving off.

Mark saw a montage flash on the screen in his peripheral vision while watching the woman leave. Brian tugged his arm, making him look at the boy, but Brian just pointed at the television with a worried look on his face. Mark followed his prompting and looked at the TV.

A picture flashed on the screen with a caption asking for the public's help. The man in the photo was wanted for questioning in the day's events. Mark stared in horror. His worst nightmare had come true. Complete and utter fear washed a chill over him. He swallowed hard. Brian grasped his hand as they both stared at the picture of Mark.

Panic rose within him as he frantically glanced at the others around him. *Good.* They were mainly still fixed on the news, and those who started to move on hadn't noticed him. Most of the people around them had blank, expressionless eyes as they stared inwardly upon their own lives in a tragic-induced zombie state.

Mark knew they better get moving before someone recognized him from that picture on the screen.

"Come on, Brian," he said, leaving the alley. The kid followed silently along as they backtracked toward Brian's father's office.

After two blocks, Brian started asking questions, which eventually led to the obvious one—why was Mark wanted for questioning? Mark had been pondering that exact question until they passed another window with another TV, and he saw a montage of his image: the train, near the bus, Park Street, and near the scene of the bike messenger. Mark wasn't sure what to tell the kid.

"Well, you gonna answer me?" Brian said, with his bluish-green eyes wide.

"Truthfully, I thought a lot about it," he said. "Now, I'm positive. The maniac is after me—and like earlier, I need to know if you can get to your father's office from here, can you?" Brian looked around, and so did Mark. "Is any of this area familiar?"

They had gone to a small park and sat on a bench. The park that was full of people just a moment before was quickly becoming a ghost town.

"Post Office square, I believe."

"Well, it kinda looks familiar," Brian said as he recognized the top of a building and the park. "Wait, this is the park with the garage under it, and that's my father's building over there. You see it? The one with the golden corners."

"I see it."

They repeated the scene from earlier but with fewer tears. Brian hugged Mark as tight as he could and thanked him before he took off running toward his father's office building. Mark hated to see the kid go, but he was surer than ever that he was and always had been the target of this whole mess, so the farther he got away from Brian and people in general, the safer everyone would be.

Ten minutes later, he was in line at Dunkin' Donuts at Haymarket station, breaking a $10 bill so he could use the machine to get a ticket for the bus. A few minutes later, he got his change in dollar coins and boarded the first bus that was leaving, and it didn't matter where it was going as long as it would get him and the man out of town. The man had to be watching. He glanced around, wondering where the man was perched. On the way to the back of the bus, he searched each passenger's face. For now, he was satisfied, so he took his seat. So far, so good.

12

FIFTH ATTACK

The clouds rolled away, and the sky brightened over the tall buildings. Brian looked at the sky and smiled as he ran. The main entrance to his dad's office building was now visible. He pumped his legs harder. His heart pounded faster and harder than his feet hit the cement. Quickly, he reached the entrance—the door opening automatically. He rushed inside, past the security desk, to the bank of elevators. He pressed the call button for tnumber seven, his lucky number, and it was the car he used every time he came to his father's office. During most weeks, it would be at least twice.

His heart still frantically jumped up and down inside his chest. Brian's mind would not settle down. It was a confusion of images, of the terror he had just experienced. Impatiently, he waited for the elevator to open. So, he got caught up in his agonizing thoughts and didn't notice he started to do the pee-pee dance. His legs moved inward at awkward angles. There was a restroom across from the elevators, so we quickly crossed the hall to the bathroom.

The restroom was empty. Brian barely reached the urinal before his bladder burst all over the front of his chinos. He stood there as he relieved himself. His shoulders relaxed a bit, but only slightly. The stream of urine seemed to be endless. Maybe everything was going to be okay after all. Being so close to his father made him start to relax a little more—

A loud roar ripped through the building, shaking it to its metal skeleton. Brian jumped back about a foot, pissing all over himself.

"Fuck!" He yelled and looked around like he'd get in trouble for swearing. Then he continued to relieve himself. *Now what?* He knew it was another explosion. Somewhere above him. He was more frightened than ever. He wished Mark was there—and he really wanted his father. Smoke started to come from under the restroom door. Not wanting to deal with the situation, he went to the sink and washed his hands. He even splashed water onto his pants where he had wet them and tried to use the hand blower to dry them, but all he was really doing was trying to delay the inevitable—leaving the bathroom. He ran out of excuses and headed out the door.

People scrambled about, and firefighters were already in the elevator bank area, which surprised him. Wow, they got there really quick. Why? Had he been stalling for longer than he had thought? One of the firefighters saw him, grabbed his arm, and escorted him through the thick smoke to the outside. As he passed the bank of elevators,

Brian's fears kicked into overdrive. He was suddenly scared, shitless. Several firefighters were spraying into one of the elevator doors—the number seven car.

The elevator he'd always used. The one he'd stepped into, then back out again. Bile rose along with a rock in his throat. He suddenly felt light-headed, and his vision faded momentarily to black. He felt strong hands pull him upright. The firefighter said something indistinguishable. Brian and the firefighter headed out of the lobby into the light.

The bright sun momentarily blinded him before it disappeared behind clouds again. Brian coughed from the smoke inhalation. Once they cleared the doorway, the firemen spoke.

"You, all right?" He said, peering down at Brian from behind his mask.

"Yeah, I think so," Brian replied, then smiled. "Thank you." The firefighter told him to go see the paramedics, but he walked over to a stone bench and sat down. He looked around, fear washing over him, sure he would see the man chasing them. His fears changed to other thoughts: Is my dad all right? Where's Mark? Is he dead? And if Mark was, was that the reason the man now tried to kill him? Dammit, the guy almost succeeded, didn't he?

Brian couldn't take it anymore, put his head between his legs, as only children can, and started bawling into his hands. Head buried in his arms on his lap—Brian didn't notice a man, who looked distraught, just beyond the yellow police tape smile. Nor did the man see him.

Just a fucking cockroach

13

ABOUT TIME

The rain, which had been on and off all morning, stopped. The sun tried its best to shine. Parker kept an eye on the building's main entrance across the street as he sat in a window seat in a small coffee shop. The building had two entries—he just hoped this was the right one. Then Parker saw the kid running down the street next to the building. He started to follow and smiled as he recognized the boy. Where was Mark? Did he have enough and ditch the poor kid? No, that wasn't the Mark he knew. They split up as they had done earlier. What was the reason for it? He didn't know.

Parker observed Brian reach the lobby entrance, pass through security, and walk to the elevators. That's right, you little brat. *Press the button and wait for lucky old number seven.* From his position, he could see the number seven perfectly. Though he could only see that side of the elevator bank, he knew Brian would use that car. Over the last several months, not once did he use a different one.

He prayed quietly when the number five car's doors opened. And he felt extreme relief when the doors closed without Brian on board. Shortly after, five's doors closed, number seven opened, and Brian stepped inside. *Showtime.*

Parker drank the rest of his coffee in his cup, got up, and headed for the door as he pressed send. Never seeing Brian exit the elevator and cross out of sight. A few moments later, an explosion erupted across the street. Several windows blew out. A second explosion followed. People ran, screaming from the building as smoke billowed out of the doors and exploded windows above.

Parker ran out the door, pretending to be shocked. "What's this world coming to? We're not safe—anymore."

"No...no more..." someone next to him agreed.

He brought his hands to his face to hide the smile he couldn't contain. As he watched the scene in front of him unfold, television trucks appeared out of nowhere. The networks greedily waited to scoop the next breaking news story. Today would be a significant event to cover for sure. Replayed over and over to death for weeks. He watched intently as the firefighters brought people outside to safety. He stood at the edge of the—Caution Police Do Not Cross—tape. A firefighter emerged carrying a child in tan pants. The child's face was blackened with soot, so he couldn't tell whether it was a boy or girl, never mind if it was Brian. He rushed off down the police line toward an ambulance. He made it halfway when the child's head popped up over the fireman's shoulders—it was a boy—but not Brian. He smiled inwardly, relieved as he continued to watch the scene as body bags started to be brought out.

Firefighters escorted people, young and old, out of the building.

Several people died, including a child.

He was satisfied.

Yet, he never noticed the firefighter bring Brian out. Nor did he notice the cameraman behind him filming the scene. Brian now sat on the stone bench, head in his lap, crying not but 20 feet from him.

A surge of gratifying justice coursed through his well-being. "Now it's your turn to suffer. To feel what I feel…every… fucking day. Justice has been served.

14

TOO LATE

The bus pulled out of the station, and a few minutes later, they passed the Boston Museum of Science and headed toward Somerville. He should've gone north, not west. That feeling of trouble—something wrong—still stomped around like a little kid in the back of his brain. He watched the streets, the people, and the buildings go by his window. He sat in the far back. The bus was pretty empty—half the reason he chose it. A 20-something-year-old sat in the seat opposite him. Mark watched the kid who was focused on the screen of his smartphone.

Mark started to think he had made a mistake. He hoped Brian would make it to his father's. Why didn't he stay with the kid? Hell, the building was only a couple of blocks away? Suddenly the kid with the smartphone swore.

"Fuck. Holy shit," he said, looking about but talking the no one. "They blew up an office building—"

Mark had snapped up. "What office building?"

"I'm not sure, but in the financial section of the city."

Mark got up and peered over the kid's shoulders.

"Where I'm not sure. Here can you tell," the kid said, handing the phone to Mark and continuing to talk, although Mark didn't hear a thing he said. He was too busy concentrating on the small screen.

When they showed the building, Mark knew two things: it was Brian's father's office building, and he had made a big mistake. Wasting no time, he hit the nearest stop request strip. He handed the kid back his phone and headed to the front of the bus.

It wasn't all the news footage revealed. Mark saw the man. He watched the chaotic scene unfold as he had on the train platform at the first explosion. Mark's blood boiled. The man smiled. He was actually smiling ear to ear like a kid in a candy shop because he believed he had killed Brian. Rage filled his head.

Along with disgust and revenge. What sick and twisted person could kill a kid? But he already knew the answer—hell, he'd been locked up with plenty of them. He knew what kind of person it took and didn't like it. *Not one bit.*

But as the man turned to walk away, Mark saw something the man obviously didn't because he wouldn't have been smiling—Brian. He saw him sitting on a bench with his head on his lap, apparently bawling his eyes out. *Poor kid.* He had to get back to Brian as fast as he could. The bus pulled over, and he got out and waited for it to pass, then crossed the street. He hailed the first taxi he saw, only milliseconds from when his foot touched the curb's edge. The cab pulled over, and he jumped inside.

"Where to?" The cabbie asked.

"The financial district, over near State Street.

"Got it," the driver said, and they were off.

Mark hoped he'd get there in time

Traffic was heavy, but when they made it to the financial district, it was downright clogged. Total congestive disorder. The block where the office building and last attack took place was blocked off to traffic. The cab driver got Mark as close as he could. Dropping him off two blocks from the street, Mark paid the driver and then took off running. He had taken off so fast that to others, it must've looked as though he had just robbed or ditched the cab.

Mark covered the two blocks in under two minutes and made it to the cordoned-off area around the entrance in under 30 seconds. He scanned the area, looking for the bench, but saw nobody: no Brian. No man. But something had clicked into place back on the bus—while he saw the man smile. Without a doubt, Mark knew that smile, but somehow it just didn't fit the face. Still, there was something he missed.

His heart hammered away in his chest. He had made a grave mistake that may have cost the kid's life. Mark knew that was definitely, something he couldn't live with. On the tiny screen, he saw smoke coming out of the entranceway of the building. Now, only a faint smell of smoke remained. He walked up to the nearest firefighter.

"Excuse me. They let people go back inside?"

"Yes, but only workers."

"There was a boy," he pointed toward the stone bench, "sitting over there. Have you seen him?"

"Yeah, I know the kid; his father works here…." He took a deep breath. "…I'm the one who pulled him out. I'm not sure, but think I saw him go back inside."

"Was he with anyone?"

The fireman shook his head. "Don't think so, no."

"All right, thanks," Mark said before he took off. He knew Brian really wanted to see his dad. But did the man spot him first and realize he didn't finish the job? What if Brian spotted the dude and made a break for it? Mark wasn't even sure what the fuck floor Brian's father's office was on. He looked up at the tall building, remembering something. It was at least 30 stories. Now that he thought about it, Brian did tell him during one of his rambling attacks. The 17th floor popped into his head. And he knew for sure it was the right floor. But he also knew he didn't have enough time to make it up there and back down without wasting a ton of time.

He looked around, up the street, down the street, and even looked for alleys. Someplace a kid could take off to if he panicked. Didn't see anything. Then a flash of movement caught his eye from down the street on the opposite end from which he had come. He looked intensely in that direction in time to see a flash of color. Blue. Was that the color the man was wearing? It wasn't the color Brian wore. Following his intuition—he took off in that direction.

15

OH, SNAP, BRIAN

Brian bawled until he couldn't bawl no more. Oblivious to the happenings around him, he kept his head in his lap and thought he could take a nap right there—feeling safe—with all the police and firefighters around. Then he realized they would evacuate the building soon…and…he really wanted his dad. He lifted his head, sitting up straight, as he glanced around. People were already being evacuated from the building. He searched each person's face in the area out front of the building as it filled up. He searched for his father. No luck. Disappointment hit his chest when he didn't find his dad.

Brian knew that he could have exited through a different exit or that his father was on the other side of the caution tape. He searched faces. The cameraman drew his attention, but the man in front of him held it—the man. He wore a different jacket, this one blue. *Scared.* He shrunk behind the bench. Suddenly not feeling so safe, even would all the police around.

Instead of telling the nearest police officer.... His fight-or-flight response kicked in—he ran—straight through the crowd and under the caution tape, just yards behind the man. He was sure. Positive, he had been seen. He almost reached an alley next to the building when a powerful set of hands grabbed him by the scruff—and—turned him around.

"Fucking cockroach," Parker said. "Can't you just die?" He dragged Brian behind a news van that blocked the entrance to an alley. He checked to make sure nobody would see him as he took matters into his own fucking hands. Strangling the kid wasn't part of the plan. Truthfully, he wasn't sure if he could, but what choice did he have, really? *None.* Not that he could think of. *Fuck*, he screamed in his head. Someone was coming. A man ran full steam up the street from the other end toward them.

Fear suddenly washed over him, recognizing the man as he got closer, making him furious.

"Come on," he bellowed, pulling the boy back through the crowd. "Make a peep. Say anything, and I'll kill you right here," he whispered in his ear.

Parker then thought *cockroaches.* He took a glance back at the running man. *Fucking cockroaches.* Mark would still have to play his game. Now that Mark was here—he could get rid of them both. *Wouldn't that be fun,* he thought as he dragged Brian down a narrow side street, his coat ruffling from a cold breeze that washed past them.

16

CHASE

With his heart pounding in his chest, Mark rushed to where he saw the flash of hurried movement at the far edge of the 30-story building. He turned the corner onto a small alley-like street. One that was a little bit wider than a box truck. Tall buildings loomed overhead. Ominous sentinels blocked out what little sunlight emanated from the hidden sky.

A cool breeze swept toward him, sending a chill crawling up his spine and a sudden blast of fear. He had to find Brian. The explosion almost blew him to bits. It worked if this was the man's way of getting to Mark. *Without a doubt.*

He proceeded into the darkened street, avoiding puddles that pooled in the narrow, cracked, and beaten sidewalk. Mark could see far enough ahead to know the street turned to the right at the base of a tall granite office building. Feeling a bit uneasy, he stepped into the middle of the street and continued onward—a moment later, he heard a high-pitched screech. A kid's scream. Throwing caution out the window, he took off at full throttle toward the sound of the cry for help. Not his best decision. Probably one he would regret. As he barreled around the corner, he was struck by an eerie silence. *Panic screamed inside his head.* Too late.

An explosion erupted from behind him—the blast knocking him down to the ground. Fire spread across the slick street, blocking his way back. He had no choice but to proceed. He looked down the narrow street toward his only escape, but scanned the road and the buildings looking for another way out. As he scrambled to his feet, he noticed the trash cans at the edge of the sidewalk on both sides of the street. Trash cans were placed every few yards from one another. The fire behind him licked the sky. He could feel the intense heat grow.

The fire moved toward him, so he had a decision to make. The street glimmered with a slick greenish color. Fuck! The panic inside his head was back, screaming louder for him to get out. *Now!*

A flash of light made him shut his eyes before a deafening sound pounded his eardrums, and the blast's shockwave knocked him back down. Fire now came for him in two directions. His ears rang, and his eyes burned. He staggered down the street. Smoke impaired his vision enough to crash into something hard. A pole. Then something round—a trashcan. The man was toying with him. He could have killed him already. Why didn't he? Questions without answers swirled around in his mind. Another explosion. This time in front of him. The fire now encroached from three directions.

Not a pleasant way to die. Mark felt the man meant to torture him alive. Using fire was definitely an excellent way to do it. He hugged the building, searching for another way out, a window or door, as he moved toward the new blaze in front of him—obscured by the thickening smoke that billowed around him. He got as close to the ground as he could in a half-crouch. He inched forward with one hand on the building. Another can exploded somewhere off to his left. An indistinguishable scream passed through the din of the low rumble of the encroaching flames. It came again. Unmistakably clear—

"Mark! No. Mark!"

Hearing Brian scream for him while in a state of self-doubt made Mark cringe with the vilest disgust. He pounded his fist on the wall. On the ground. Back on the wall. This time he was rewarded with the unmistakable sound of vibrating glass. Mark reluctantly smiled; he had found a window. A way out. It was about two feet from the ground. A slit of glass about four feet long and maybe four feet wide. *It was gonna be a tight fit, but what choice did he have?*

He stepped away from the window and then off the curb, and with every bit of his weakening strength, he launched himself at the winking window. Glass tingled in a cascade of different tones as he crashed through—and fell eight feet to the cement floor below. The impact forced air out of his lungs. Glass rained down around him.

Pain bloomed throughout his wrecked body. His already hurt leg now throbbed with pain. Another, more acute, pain alighted in his left forearm. A four-inch sliver of glass protruded from his skin. He pulled it out with total indifference as blood gushed from the wound, soaking his sleeve.

He glanced around the room and found himself in what appeared to be a laundry. Stacks of neatly folded shirts were piled upon several countertops: corporate T-shirts. He took one, tore it into threads, and tied off his arm and leg. Once that was done, he looked for an exit.

Brian still lived, so I didn't have to kill the guy, though he still might—and that meant he still had work to do. At first, Mark believed one hundred percent, beyond any doubt, that the man was only using Brian to draw him out, but now he could see he was wrong. *Totally.* The man was using him to flush Brian out into the open. *Fuck*, how could he be so stupid? All along, Brian was the target. He had to be. It made sense. But why would anyone want to murder a kid like Brian? Any kid, for that matter. What could he have done—it felt like too extreme a measure to kill a child? None of it made any sense. None whatsoever. When did violence ever, anyhow? Mark couldn't think of any time it had—even in war.

In a dazed state of confusion, it took him several minutes to find a stairwell and climb the two flights to the main level for what seemed like forever. His head ached and made his vision wonky. A slow process with a bad leg. He came to a door on the second-floor landing and found a two-story entranceway lined with windows along one side. The floor-to-ceiling windows reached some 30 feet above. The effect was awe-inspiring.

He glanced around, searching for any way out. But he saw no exit to the world beyond the windows. He also realized he was at the far end of the building. At the opposite end of the space, Mark could see people milling about in a lobby. He moved in that direction and made it less than five measly feet when a flurry of movement outside rushed past the window—the kid. An adult hot on his heels. Brian. *Shit!* He took off in a lumbering pursuit. The pain he felt was now forgotten.

When he approached the lobby, a guard appeared out of nowhere and held up his hand for him to stop. Mark could feel the man's gaze scrutinizing the way Mark looked. He knew he made one helluva sight, and the guard wondered what he was doing there. Reluctantly, Mark stopped. *He didn't have time for this.* Brian needed him—

"Excuse me, sir," the contempt was apparent in the guard's voice. "Where're you going in such a rush?"

His mind flooded with images: the narrow escape from the fire, the blood soaking through his clothing, and Brian almost being blown to dust and led away by the man. The man who would undoubtedly strap a bomb to the poor kid and finish what he started. The thought made Mark sick. He looked past the guard—to the last spot he had seen Brian. Just saw Brian being caught by the man and dragged off out of sight.

"I was just leaving."

"I'm going to have to ask you to come with me."

"For what?"

"Sir, calm down and just tell me where you just came from?"

Mark thought as quickly as his preoccupied mind would allow. "This is un-fucking-believable. I just had the worst morning of my life—almost got blown to fucking pieces. Twice. On a fucking train." The guard's eyes went wide in surprise. "Look at me. I look like bloody fucking hell. And… where was I…coming from—None of your fucking business!

But if you really must know, my attorney's office." Mark just prayed to God there was a lawyer's office in the building.

The guard stood there, slack-jawed, believing he had just made a mistake.

Mark pushed past the stunned guard, not giving the guard a chance to speak. Luckily, the guard let him go without protest. The bombings had been all over the news—continuous coverage. Without looking back, Mark headed out of the exit. The moment he passed the spot where he last saw Brian—he started running in the direction he perceived they had gone. He ran two blocks, glancing down each street, alley, or doorway he passed. As he stopped to catch his breath, he was panting heavily. He pulled fresh, refreshing air into his lungs. As he did, he saw a man walking ahead of him with a petulant child. He smiled—a sinister smile.

Though the area had changed drastically while he was in prison, Mark knew the man was headed out of the financial district, but to where he wasn't sure—until he found himself cutting through the park where the raised highway had long since been removed. The man, still in sight, seemed to take Brian somewhere in South Boston. As to confirm this, he saw them cross the walkable bridge to Southie. Though it had been many years, this section of the city known as the Seaport District was now home to new hotels, the convention center, new housing highrises, and of course, warehouses leftover from before gentrification took over the district.

17

MAKE A RUN FOR IT

The man gripped Brian by the collar and led him into the narrow alley. A gust of cool air brushed past them. Brian shivered but wasn't sure of the cause—whether, from the cold or the evil man, he didn't know. But the scary man had already killed many people and tried to kill him. He felt helpless as the man's powerful grip guided him deeper into the shadows of the alley. *Where's Mark?* He wished he was there to save him. There was no doubt in his mind that he was a goner.

He thought the man would kill him once they were out of sight, but that didn't happen. They neared the elbow of the street as it turned to the right and deeper, still into the shadows cast by the buildings surrounding them. What was he waiting for? There had to be a reason, but his frightened mind couldn't quite comprehend what it could be.

Brian heard a ZZZZEEE sound that seemed to get louder. The man seemed not to notice. And he knew some kids used to use certain sounds for ring tones because those over 30 couldn't hear specific frequencies. When they got closer to the elbow, without warning, the sound changed to a guttural ZZRZRRZZ sound—and a figure zipped around the corner of the narrow street.

Caught by surprise, the man released his grip. Brian bolted to the opposite side of the street as the man dove to the other. Using this opportunity, Brian ran around the corner, searching for a place to hide. This part of the street was wider. A tall building that reached high into the sky, making him dizzy as he looked up, took up most of the left side of the street.

On the right, he saw another alley, barely big enough for him to squeeze down, between the two buildings that made up the right-side street. He tucked his arms in front of him and shuffled into the space, knowing the man couldn't fit. At the end of the alley, it opened up to a courtyard of sorts. It opened up to the left, where a fire escape ran to the top of the several-story building. The other building had several doors. He tried with no luck. He sat on a milk crate he grabbed from a stack of them just outside one of the doors.

"Brian! Brian!" the man called.

He swallowed hard, stood up, walked to the edge of the building, and peered down the alleyway toward the street— in time to see the man pass by.

"Brian!" the man called again.

Bile rose in Brian's throat. How did he know his name? The man repeatedly called for him—then nothing but silence. One so eerie it made the hackles on the back of his neck and the hair on his arm stand up.

"We've got company, Brian," the man called in a giddy tone. "I guess…I'll just play with him a little bit."

Who are you talking about, Brian thought?

"It's Mark…Brian," the man laughed hysterically. "He's come to save you. The Savior of Little Brats. But who is going to save him, Brian?" The man's sinister laughter echoed down the alley and into the courtyard, making it even more ominous. "Don't worry. I set up a very nice greeting for him. One you're gonna love."

Brian sat back down on the crate and bawled his eyes out. He couldn't hold back any longer. How could he save Mark? Was he really coming? Or was it what do you call it—a ploy? Brian didn't know, so we looked for another way out, but there was only the fire escape. It was too high off the ground for him to pull it down, even with the help of four crates. So, he'd be stuck there until the man gave up, which Brian knew would never happen. No matter how much he bawled or prayed.

The air in the small courtyard changed as he heard a loud bang and whoosh. He could hear something crackling like wood on a fire. It reminded him of the fireplace at home. Then he smelled…smoke. He understood that the man's welcome wagon had just greeted Mark.

He squeezed down the narrow passage and watched Mark get up and continue to walk toward him, but on the opposite side of the street. He was about to run to Mark when a trash barrel somewhere to his left exploded. Smoke quickly filled the narrow street, blackening his view of Mark. Another exploded directly across from where he stood.

He screamed!

Tears ran silently down his face. Brian couldn't see Mark through the smoke because it was too thick. He was afraid Mark was dead—then he heard a crash, someone cursing. Mark. A smile flashed on his face, but quickly as it came, it left. Another explosion off to his left erupted.

Brian realized for the first time his ears were ringing, and the street filled up with thick, black smoke. He coughed and hacked from the choking air. He couldn't see much before, but now he saw nothing. Inches in front of him. Tears blurred his vision—and he screamed his worry once more.

"Mark! No…" He screamed. As soon as he did it again, he realized it was a mistake. A dark figure filled the entrance of the passage. Powerful hands groped out of the billowing smoke, trying to grasp hold of him. He pushed hard and ran out of the narrow alley. He broke to the right when the fire was smoldering, and the smoke was not as black. He knew that was the way out—the only way.

18

WAREHOUSE

"You want to get out now?" the taxi driver questioned. "Here?"

"Yes, thank you," he said, handing the man $30. "Keep the change."

"If you say so, but that leg must be killing you to spend $30 for a less than a three-block ride."

Seeing it as a way out, Mark agreed.

Mark exited the cab with haste and looked in the direction he had come. They had passed Brian and the man a block or so back. Brian looked terrified. Mark could make them out now as they came into view. He feared he lost them for a moment, that they would have turned off before Mark could get out of the cab.

Though he was pleased to see them headed his way, he didn't understand why the guy hadn't killed Brian yet. If Brian was indeed the target, why hadn't he? The question nagged at him as he walked to the nearest building and posted up inside a doorway—and watched as they approached.

A block to go.

Despite eyes peeled in that direction, he blinked and almost lost sight of them. He blinked again, wincing from the pain—and they were gone. *Shit!*

Mark cursed himself some more as he headed toward where he lost sight of them. He should've known it wasn't going to be that easy. A few minutes later, he stood at the spot. The foot traffic in the area had been light, so he was sure he hadn't passed them. He even looked in the few shop windows and alleys he passed. Then, acting solely on instinct, he went down the first alley.

The alley was littered with trash, dumpsters, milk crates, and other various debris, making it hard to navigate. Maneuvering through all the junk would be impossible at any speed. If they had come this way, he should spot them soon. He just hoped he didn't have to return this way after getting Brian. They would be caught for sure. The narrow passageway snaked, zigzagging, behind storefronts to three, as far as he could tell, warehouses.

Like the tall buildings, the sunlight present before entering the alley was all but forgotten. The place gave him the creeps—and his intuition screamed: Danger! *Danger Will Robinson* repeatedly in his head. Somewhere up ahead, just out of sight, a door slammed shut. He had to be getting close. He could feel it…deep in his bones. A giant fat rat scurried across his path, scaring the living bejesus out of him. He chuckled at himself because the man he was chasing was far scarier than a rat—even a big fat one.

Before he got them both killed, he had to keep his nerves in check. He took a deep breath, bringing it through his nose as he quietly chanted, stay calm, stay calm. He stopped at the next corner and peered around. Nobody. There was indeed a door for the building on the right. Silently, he crept his way to the door. Tried the knob, and to his surprise, it twisted all the way. He pulled, and the door swung outward. Silently on greased hinges. Beyond the door, it was nothing but pitch blackness.

The black hole gaped at him. He swallowed hard, ignoring the warning alarms going off inside his skull, and entered the building. Beyond the threshold, a wide corridor led further into the darkness. There were two doors on each side of the hallway. At the end, it split into two directions in a T section. He passed the four doors, stopped in the middle of the split, looked in both directions, and then back at the doors he didn't check.

Knowing he might regret it later, he turned back and checked the first room on his right. Empty. The one across from it was also empty. He walked across the hall to the next door, and as he did so, he heard a loud crash and then a scream. However, not that of a child. The person was now cursing. It sounded like it came from somewhere above him, but he wasn't sure. He didn't bother to check the other two rooms. He turned left at the split and walked along the doorless corridor. A doorway at the end opened to a vast room one would expect to find in a warehouse.

Rows and rows of pallets and shrink-wrapped boxes. Stacked high as the ceiling would allow—maybe 20 or 30 feet. Boxes were stacked at the head of each column, along every wall, and space between. A virtual labyrinth. The voice that was embedded in his skull came back—*danger*.

Mark made his way to the nearest aisle and was halfway to the end when he heard another crash. This one was definitely from upstairs, directly above him. A moment later, he heard a loud, indistinguishable bellow. A door slammed, hurried, heavy footfall, and another door slammed. Probably the same one. It was hard to tell.

Again, with the bellowing, this time more clearly: "Where you going, you little dumb shit? Do you even know the way out? I doubt it. I blindfolded you; don't you remember? Come on, you little bastard—show yourself."

Silence.

Mark stopped moving as if not to make a sound.

"Better yet, stay here! As a matter of fact, Jack, that's a better idea. Thanks for giving it to me."

Mark strained to listen; although the man was yelling, it was still a flight above. He could hear clearly, but it was like loud talking from a distance too great. But that voice. The speech pattern sounded familiar. He was sure he knew that voice. He wasn't wrong about that, and as if the man had read his mind.

"Mark ain't gonna save you, boy. He's roast beef by now. Too bad, I really liked that son of a bitch. He was a good man. Too good for his own good. Just you and me in here, boy—and soon it'll just be you."

Another crash.

"Fuck. Think you're slick, you little bastard. I almost broke my neck on that twine you strung across. Very clever. A fucking regular MacGyver, we got here, don't we? But I made it to my exit boy, so long. Have fun—with all the charges I've set in here, boy. Oh, it's gonna be a hell of a blast. And you and the rats in this place won't survive. No way. See you around— just kidding."

Another door, heavier than the last, slammed shut. Did he really leave? Or was it just a ploy to get Brian to reveal himself? How did he lose the kid? Mark made it almost to the other end. He could hear heavy footfall descending creaky wooden steps—the stairs groaned in protest at the man's weight. Kieth jogged in the direction of the stairs, protesting screams.

The building became terribly silent.

Though against his better judgment, he continued to move toward where he believed the man would come out. On the other side of the building, Mark found a door that led to a hallway to what looked like the office for the warehouse. He made it five feet down the hallway when something swung out of the darkness and crashed into his chest, sending him to the ground. Bells started ringing—and not just inside his head. Actual bells. Stars twinkled in front of his eyes.

He heard the man's voice rumble like a 30-foot wave crashing to the shore. "Shit. Fuck. Who could that be…who's there?"

Mark lay there in silence. His vision started to focus as it adjusted to the darkness. The only sound came from the pendulum swinging back and forth above his head. The object that struck him down. He felt as though he got hit with a ton of bricks. Mark regained his vision. *Figures*, he thought as he watched the heavy bag continue its arc above him. He rolled out of the way. But not in time—

Strong hands grabbed him from behind as he tried to crawl into the nearest room.

"Oh, no, you don't," the man growled, lifting him effortlessly off the ground before slamming him into the nearest wall. Mark's body making a deep impression in the drywall. Air rushed from his lungs. Mark could feel the man's hot breath on his face. But the darkness made it difficult to determine the man's facial features.

"What are you doing here?"

Mark stayed silent.

The man's powerful arms slammed him into the opposite wall. Mark grunted as pain exploded sharply from his back. This time, he had hit a stud. Mark remembered something—the man knew him.

"It's me," he said, barely audible. "It's me…Mark."

"Mark?" the man said, relaxing his grip slightly.

Mark made his move and smashed his head into the man's nose. He grabbed him by the shoulders and pulled them down while simultaneously bringing up his knee with all his might. Mark's knee crashed precisely into the man's solar plexus, who grunted in pain on impact. Mark repeated the move two more times. Then pushed the man back, making him backpedal a few steps.

"You gotta do better than Th—"

Mark leapt off the ground, spun backward 180°, and shot out his foot in a perfectly executed jumping back kick, catching the man in his chest. A little high. But he sent the man flying off his feet and crashing through the wall behind him. The man landed hard on the floor, unconscious.

Mark stumbled up the stairwell in the direction he believed Parker had come from. Once he made it to a steel door with no keyhole, Mark called for Brian but no reply. He kept calling. Eventually, he heard movement beyond the door.

"Come on—we need to get out of here—now," he called through the door.

Mark heard a noise behind him and spun on his heels, ready for action. Nobody.

Brian climbed out from behind a row of pallets. "You're alive—"

Brian ran to the sound of Mark's voice and the door.

"Mark, is that really you?" Brian said in an excited voice. "I can't open the door. There is no lock on this side."

"Stand away from the door."

"Okay, I'm away from the door."

"Good," Mark said as he threw all his weight at the door. It didn't budge. He stepped back and threw a front kick to the door, just under the doorknob. *Nothing.* Not wanting to waste more time, he had an idea. "Brian, is there anything to the right of the door?"

"My right? No. Nothing."

Stand back.

He didn't wait for a reply and kicked a hole in the drywall next to the left side of the door. He cleared the hole out, making it big enough for Brian to get through. After ensuring no wires or whatever was in the way, Mark kicked through the other side.

Brian squeezed through the tight space and into the stairwell. Mark pulled him to his feet and hugged the kid. As they went down the stairs, Mark motioned Brian to be quiet.

When they made it to the first-floor landing where Mark had left the man—they found the spot empty. The man had vanished.

Brian looked at the debris on the floor and the body-sized holes in the walls. "What happened here?"

"I almost died."

Brian swallowed noisily.

"I'm sorry, little man, it was just a fight, and luckily, I came out on top. Barely. But I did, nevertheless. I don't see an exit, do you?"

Brian shook his head. "Um…no…I don't."

"Then we're gonna have to go out the same way we came in."

Brian followed Mark across the big room, snaking around boxes. The route took them by a row of oversized, grimy, dirty windows. The warehouse groaned. An eerie sound. And Mark didn't like it, and neither did Brian. Suddenly, the place became calm. Too quiet. Everything, including the dust motes, seemed for a moment to stand still. *This ain't good.*

He grabbed Brian, held him tight to his chest and turned his back toward the windows, and started to crouch—

The room erupted in a bright light. The force of the explosion blew out all the windows and parts of the building.

The blinding white light lifted them off the ground and through the windows. Mark opened his eyes. All around him looked like a war-torn country. He could not move, something pinned him to the ground, but he could move his arms and wiggle his fingers.

Incoherent whimpering. *Where's Brian?* It took all his energy to move his head to look down, but he did. There, Brian hugged him tightly. Brian. Mark tried to speak…but nothing came out. Brian looked a little beaten up but otherwise unharmed from what he could tell.

Mark mustered all the strength he could. "I'm okay, Brian." Everything faded to black as he passed out.

19

LIL BASTARD

The fire engulfed most of the street. Parker felt elated. No way Mark could have survived, but he had thought that before. He smiled to himself. *Pleased.* He could hear the brat calling for Mark. He knew putting Mark in danger would draw Brian out into the open. His smile broadened because it worked. Parker left his perch on top of the building next to the slit of an alley. He knew Brian was back there somewhere, but he was too wide for the passage.

He climbed down a sturdy fire escape, dropped to the ground, walked the five paces to the alley—and blocked the entrance with his sheer girth. Brian was already standing at the entrance, so Parker grabbed him. Thick black smothering smoke billowed around him, making him miss. Small hands with surprising power pushed him off balance. He stumbled but did not fall. He felt the brat rush past him, and it took a moment for him to spot the kid in the murkiness.

Parker glanced back at the fire as it raged. Satisfied it would take care of Mark, he ran after the brat. The lil bastard was quick. He knew the kid headed away from the blaze to the other end of the street. That's right...little man...save yourself. He watched the kid disappear back into the smoke.

Parker checked left and right at the end of the street before turning right and heading back toward Brian's father's office building. Sirens pierced the air but had actually never stopped. The sound was constant this morning.

Parker mused that people would remember this day. He stopped and glanced back over his shoulder. *Nothing.* He walked another ten feet, and the feeling he was going in the wrong direction overwhelmed him so much he turned around. And as he did, he saw the kid standing at the end of the street. The kid also spotted Parker, who smiled and ran in the opposite direction Parker had initially gone. *Smug brat.* Parker gave chase.

Huge skyscrapers took up most of the street. Brian screamed bloody blue murder as he ran. People stopped and stared. Eventually, Parker caught up to him—and snatched him up by the caller as onlookers watched in total disgust. Brian immediately took advantage of the situation.

"Let go! Let...go...of me, now!" Brian screamed as he tried to pull away. "This ain't my dad! I don't know this guy."

Parker's eyes flared furiously. He glanced around. The onlookers were now looking at him in disgust. A short woman, perhaps in her twenties, spoke first—and he knew this wasn't good.

"Let that...little boy...Go!" She yelled.

"Yeah, like the lady said, dude, let him go," a deep baritone voice instructed from behind him.

Parker turned to see a huge musclebound man, who stood easily 6' 5" and took up most of the 5-foot-wide sidewalk. Parker let go of the kid, then tried to talk himself out of the situation.

Brian stood there for a moment, confused.

"Hey, kid, did he try to touch you?" A man in a business suit inquired.

Brian looked at him. "No, but I think he wanted to."

Parker scowled at Brian.

"Someone, call the police," Brian said but hesitated, "he tried to kill me."

His comment, one made on a day like this one, seemed over the top. Brian could tell they didn't believe him. Then he added lamely, "he's the bomber!"

"That ain't funny," someone said. Brian could feel the current change against him. Seeing where this was headed, Brian took off. Never looking back.

Parker suppressed a smile, knowing the kid just helped him. Quickly he explained that Brian's father was a lawyer who works in the building where a bomb had just gone off—and that he was supposed to watch the kid, but he'd taken off on him. The bystanders apologized, and Parker, once again, gave chase.

Brian didn't make it far. Parker saw the kid turn left and caught up to him before he reached the opposite corner. There was not a soul to interfere on the side street.

"You can make all the noise you want now," Parker sneered. "Ain't no one around to listen.

"Where're you taking me?"

"Shut up," Parker snapped. "The quieter you are, the longer you live."

Brian, who didn't want to cry in front of such a monster, couldn't help himself as he bawled.

The streets around the building were completely deserted. Parker hoped he didn't waste the last of the explosive disks on Mark. That guy and this kid were harder to kill than cockroaches, but he'd bring the brat to the warehouse. Where he had more explosives—and it would, at last, be a big blast. *Once and for all.*

Brian tried to pull away, and Parker cuffed him in the back of the head. "Stop it, or I'll snap your fucking little neck. Got it?" Parker looked down at the boy, who stared up at him with pleading eyes. "Sorry, kid, I ain't the one." Parker loosened his grip a little, and Brian stopped fighting.

Brian wished for Mark to save him. It had worked earlier, so Brian believed. He even asked for a sign. The sun had retreated, and the entire sky had become a dark gray that the sun's rays could not penetrate. However, when Brian looked up to the sky, the clouds broke, and the sun peeked out briefly—then it was gone. Brian smiled. Mark ain't dead. *No way.* But the man was gonna wish he was.

When they made it to the bridge, Parker looked back to make sure he wasn't being followed. There were a couple of people behind him and several more back at the park, but no Mark in sight, and that was all he really cared about. *Stay dead, cockroach. Stay dead.*

There were a couple more blocks to go before they would be at the warehouse, where no one would find them. Parker picked up his pace. "Come on, pick it up!"

Parker thought back to when he and Mark were in prison together. The good old days. Parker remembered it well. Mark used to come to this kid's aid every time he tried to catch a little rec. "Yo, little man...don't pay Parker no mind. I don't" Then he'd walk off with the kid in tow. Although Parker was a big man, he knew better than to go toe to toe with Mark. He'd seen the man in action—it was brutal. Mark had a good heart and looked out for people. Parker came to suspect that's why he felt somewhat bad about offing him. *Good guys, finish last.* Didn't your mother ever teach you that? Unfortunately, he picked the wrong day to play hero, or was he paying penitence for his sins? Nevertheless—it was the wrong day.

They walked two more blocks, then turned right into a trash-strewn alley. Parker expertly navigated his way through the maze of debris. An expert who had gone this route many times. Brian struggled to keep pace. Parker looked down at the boy, who was being extra quiet. He hadn't tried to get away again. He expected the boy to try, especially in the alley, but instead, he was on his best behavior.

"Why are you being so quiet?" Parker asked, coming to a stop, pulling Brian back by the collar. Almost yanking the boy off his feet. "What gives?"

Brian looked up at Parker. "Nothing. Either way, you gonna do whatever you gonna do, so I...I don't know...gave up." He lied. *Mark, please be out there.*

Parker shook his head and pushed Brian from the back in the direction they were headed. "Let's go, be careful. Wouldn't want you to slip and fall, breaking your neck," Parker said with a smile, an evil thing it was. "I'd rather do it myself."

"Then…do…it," Brian squeaked out in a small voice, "…already."

Parker cackled manically as they made the last turn and approached the only noticeable door. The door was located in the right-hand corner of the second two-story warehouse on the right. Parker pulled it open and pushed Brian inside, sending the boy to the floor. Parker entered, bent down, and pulled Brian roughly to his feet.

"Stop stalling," Parker grumbled. "You're safe, for now, anyway."

He led Brian to the end of the hall, turned right, and followed the corridor through another door into the warehouse proper. The warehouse was owned by a man who loved cars, boats, and what looked to Parker as the contents of ten garages. Parker rented the entire top floor. The only access to the second floor was on the other side of the football field length room.

The place was littered with junk, like the alley leading to the building. The building only had two exits. The one he entered and the garage bay doors to the left. Large, frosted glass brick windows let in a lot of light. Besides the cars, boats, and junk, several rows of shelving rose at least 20 feet high—and the aisles were chock full of debris.

They meandered their way to the stairs that led to the second floor. Brian stumbled and fell to the ground along the way. When they came to the door, they headed to the stairs. Parker unlocked it and went up the stairs to the second-floor landing. A heavy, shiny new steel door greeted them.

He reached for the doorknob, which had no keyhole. Parker grasped the knob, and a loud audible click alerted him the door was now unlocked. He entered his lab as he thought of it anyhow. The keyless entry was allowed by an aphid implanted just below the skin of his right wrist. It also opened and allowed the ignition to be turned in his car.

Unlike the downstairs, there was a semblance of order in the lab. Almost a dozen rooms on the second floor, and all of them had a purpose. The first room they entered was the smallest, which Parker used as his office. The place where he drafted the schematics for the disks and laid out his plan of revenge.

Just inside the room to the right, a door led to another corridor. The corridor went straight down the middle to about halfway across the second floor. Along the hallway were seven large rooms. One was empty. He assembled the disks at the one across from the office. The next one in line on the right was his bedroom, which had a bathroom with a shower. The room across the hall, and the one after it, was used for storage. He had knocked out the wall to join the two rooms. The storage room is by far the messiest. Boxes upon boxes were stacked everywhere. Three aisles of shelving almost reached the ceiling in the room. The last two rooms were empty but wouldn't be for long. The final room on the left also had a bathroom but no shower. Parker figured that room, void of any furniture, would be perfect for the little guest. He opened the door and pushed Brian into the room.

"Get comfortable, kid. We'll be here a while," he said. Brian stumbled from being pushed but did not fall. He made his way over to the only window. "Only view from that window is the brick wall, less than half a foot away."

Brian looked at the man with a blank stare.

Although Parker knew what the kid was thinking. "Don't worry, kid, you'll get to see your father again," Parker's face brightened, "but only for a moment, then he'll get to see you die—"

"Why, I'm just a kid!" Brian shouted, no longer able to hold back his emotions. "I'm just a kid!"

"So was Michael. He was just a kid…too!" Parker screamed before he slammed and locked the door.

The other half of the second floor was one giant room. Parker referred to it as the machine shop because it contained every piece of machinery a good fabrication shop needed. It was part metal and part electronic workspace. It was where he manufactured the deadly backpack devices, the disks. The manufacturing room contained enough plastic explosives to level the building and the buildings around the warehouse. The thought amused Parker and stirred something darkly deep within his soul. Life wasn't supposed to turn out this way. *Losing a child can change you.*

It can change some into complete monsters—and Parker knew that was precisely what he'd be labeled by the end of the day.

If he wanted, Parker could have left a trail that led to someone else. Mark would've been a good candidate, but it was too late to use him now, but there was someone he could blame—the rich kid that financed most of his work.

It had been a lucky day for Parker when the kid's letter arrived in the mail. Parker had lost a child. The kid, who he believed was seventeen at the time, wrote him. He turned out to be his biggest fan and believed Parker did the right thing. The courts did not see it that way. The man who murdered his son Michael was set free. Although the defense attorney claimed the man was innocent, Parker couldn't bear the insult, so a month after the man was acquitted, he became judge, jury, and executioner. In the end, Parker was convicted of murder and sentenced to life in prison without a chance of parole.

Parker was a respected engineer, a graduate from MIT, and somewhat wealthy. He lost everything in the act. His wife, the traitorous bitch, left him along with most of the 500 grand in their savings. What money his wife and her lawyer didn't take was drained by his lawyer for his trial and appeal. But in the end, he won his freedom—on a technicality. For once, a good guy got to use the loopholes in the law. As far as Parker was concerned, he didn't kill a person but a hideous monster that preyed upon the weakest members of society. *Children.*

God's work will now be done. He will wake up the people in our sleeping nation. They all believe they are safe. Not in the least. They will listen now. His act of revenge against those he held most responsible for his child's murderer to go free—and for forcing Parker to take it upon his own hands—will wake them up.

Parker left the door and walked to the other end of the corridor, where there was another heavy door. The machine shop. He entered through the door and closed it behind him with only one thought on his mind—soon, it would be over.

###

Brian sat in the corner off to the right of the door. There was only one other door leading to a windowless bathroom. He sat there with his knees to his chest as he hugged them. An hour had passed, according to his watch. After the man left, he bawled but still held onto hope. The sign wasn't wrong. Mark would come to save him. Though he had seen how intense the fire had been, he still held out hope.

When he couldn't shed another tear, he just sat there with his back to the wall and arms wrapped around his legs, put his head on his lap, and fell asleep. His short, albeit wonderful, life flashed before him like a broken recording set to repeat everything twice. Reviewing his life wasn't helping matters. No, by all accounts, it made things worse.

Brian opened his eyes and stretched his legs straight out. He got the urge to pee some time ago but didn't feel like getting up to use the bathroom. Now he really had to go. He got up and ran to the bathroom. After finishing, he washed his hands, though with no soap, and went back into his makeshift cell. He tried the door again, but it was locked. Just as it had been when he tried it earlier. Crazy thoughts jumped into his mind. The only person who could save him might be dead. Nobody else knew where he was. By now, his father must be frantic, especially after he discovered it started with the train Brian usually took into town.

Brian also knew the man's promise to kill him would happen if no one stopped him or he couldn't get away. He found it harder and harder to concentrate when he knew he would die in a few hours, not just simply stop breathing, but blown to bits in front of his father. For no reason, it made him wonder about kids his age who had terminal cancer. They lived their lives to the fullest, even though they knew they could die anytime. Brian marveled at the thought and had ever since he learned about it in health class.

His teacher, Mrs. Pratt, had two special guests come into class. A 10-year-old girl named Mary and a 13-year-old boy named Harry. Because of his current situation, he had a newfound respect for terminal cancer patients, and if he got out of this, he would do what he could. His friend Peter and his mom volunteered at Children's Hospital all the time. Maybe he could go with them. He needed to be like them and not give up.

"I'm not going to give up!" He shouted aloud to the empty room. "I will find a way out of here. I can't give up." He sucked in a deep breath and then bellowed one-word "MARK!"

He barely started when the door to the room opened… and the man barged in. "Stop making all this noise," Parker warned as he snatched Brian by the shoulders. "Nobody…is going to…hear you."

Brian took Taekwondo for a while and was in a fighting stance with his right leg back—and just smiled at Parker before releasing a front ball push kick to the man's groin, hitting his target dead center. Parker groaned. His knees bent as another kick came from the other leg. Brian hitting his Mark. Parker collapsed to the floor, though only briefly and probably more out of surprise than anything else, but it was enough time for Brian to bolt out of the room.

He ran first to the door leading to the machine shop, not remembering which way he came. He tried the knob, but it was locked, so he ran to another. In the end, he found a door on the right side that was left open. Brian recognized it as the way they had come in. He ran inside the room and found that the other door was locked with no keyhole or anything—just a doorknob. Brian didn't understand how that was possible, but maybe it was controlled by something remote.

He bolted from the room.

"Where are you, you lil bastard," bellowed the man.

Brian tried the first door he came to and went inside. The storage room.

The old building groaned. Parker sentiments exactly. He clawed his way to his feet. The kid nailed him good, but he had to admit it took courage. Luckily for him, there was no place for the boy to go. Parker could neither leave nor access the machine shop or his bedroom. He left the assembly shop door open so he could go in there, but there wasn't any place to hide. Where would he be? The office, no. Assembly, no. The empty rooms? Well, no, which left one possible place. The storage room.

"You can't go anywhere," he bellowed. There's no place to hide...I'll find you...sooner or later. But your timing couldn't be any better because I got a brand-new backpack for you. Very stylish. It's yellow, lil homie, the bomb," Parker said, then cackled. He thought he heard movement as he entered the corridor and stopped laughing.

The place became eerily quiet.

Parker searched the rooms but didn't expect to find Brian. Five minutes later, he entered the storage room and searched for the little bastard. "You have to be in here. It's the only place you can hide...I will find you."

Parker moved boxes around, even checked inside several. He then checked the top shelves as best as he could. After twenty minutes, Parker still couldn't find the kid and became angry. By the half-hour mark, he was downright pissed. He grabbed a box off the shelf to see if the kid was stowed behind it, and half of the shelf's contents came crashing down upon his head. He cursed something about the kid being a little shit. At first, he thought the kid had done it but realized that wasn't the case. It still put him on edge. He looked at his watch. *Daddy would be leaving his office in a few minutes if he hadn't already.*

There was no way he could get them to Brian's father's office within time. *Fuck it*, he thought. He can end it right here. "I guess you won't see your dad, after all, seeing you changed the plans. You can die right here." Then he stormed out of the room and went into the machine shop—and a moment later came back through the door with a yellow knapsack. He reached into the pack and started pulling out disks and tossing them two at a time into each room. When he entered the storage room, he tried to make his way to the center of the room but tripped and crashed hard to the ground. A loud whooping sound left his lungs. He sat up and saw the taut line of string across the aisle.

Nice try, kid. You gotta do better than that. Next time, oh shit, there won't be a next time." The bag landed halfway down the aisle. Parker left it there. The explosives in the pack alone would level the floor, never mind the room. Nothing could possibly survive. With his pride slightly hurt, Parker stalked out of the room and out of the second-floor makeshift apartment. He cursed the kid some more before he headed downstairs. Parker made it to the bottom landing and opened the door to the now dark hallway when he heard movement and a loud crash.

Parker waited for his eyes to adjust to the blackness. He said nothing because silence would be the best weapon in this case. Apart from the sounds of the intruder obviously in pain, he heard the chain to his heavy bag. It wasn't meant as a deterrent, but apparently, it made a good one. Hell, he had run into it in the dark many times himself.

A shadow stumbled to the right. Parker tackled the shadow. The shadow crashed heavily into the wall, leaving behind a body print. Who are you? What are you doing here? The shadow grunted in pain and shouted. "It's me, Mark." Parker stopped, shocked, his grip loosened, and Mark gained the upper hand. They scuffled, but Parker felt his body crash into the wall as everything blinked out.

20

HOSPITAL

Mark woke with a start and began screaming for Brian. "Where are you? Brian, where are you?"

A parade of doctors, orderlies, and nurses rushed into his hospital room.

Mark glanced around, realizing where he was, as a doctor approached him and told him to calm down.

"Where's Brian? There was a boy with me. Where is he?"

"He's fine. You need to rest right now. Maybe you can see him in the morning."

Mark studied the man speaking and the other faces in the room. He felt the guy was telling the truth. However, he didn't notice that one of the nurses inserted a solution into his IV bag. He shut his eyes as they got heavy.

When morning came, he asked several nurses about Brian, but nobody would tell him anything. He wasn't the bad guy: images flashed before his eyes as he remembered the TV news—this man…him…being wanted for questioning. He realized what was going on—his heart sunk.

As if to confirm his thought, two suits, a man and a woman, entered the room—cops.

Mark knew the second his eyes laid on them they were cops and regarded him as scum because he had a criminal past. He hated cops but not the good ones. There were some good ones. The type he hated hid behind their badge. The ones he liked were just doing their job. Though he knew the accusations would come, he hoped these two were those kinds of cops who wanted to help and sought the truth, not just trying to close the case as quickly as possible.

"Nobody wants to answer my question, so maybe you can. Is Brian, okay?"

"The boy's fine, but we have some questions for you," the woman said. She was tall with dark skin and a stern look. "I'm Detective Reynolds, and this is my partner, Detective Franklin."

Mark glanced at her partner. A white man with salt-and-pepper hair and a fatherly face. A face one could trust, which told Mark he needed to stay away from that one.

"Why do we have you on the scene of three different bombings?" Reynolds asked.

"Just my luck…I guess," Mark said, telling them nothing.

"What were you doing with that boy?" Franklin asked. The inflection he used for the word boy made it almost sound dirty.

Mark shook his head. "I'm sure he already told you."

The two cops exchange looks.

Mark let his head drop to the pillow. "I want an attorney."

"Lawyering up already?" Franklin said. "Got something to hide?"

"Yeah, what are you hiding?" Reynolds added.

"Nothing. The kid will tell you the only thing I did…was try my best to keep us alive."

"Yes, we know, but maybe there's more," Reynolds said in an accusatory tone.

"Look, Putz One and Putz Two," Mark spat. "I was just released this morning. If you checked, you would know—right? On the same day I am released from prison, you think I could blow up the train I was on and terrorize the city? Now, in case you didn't hear me the first time. I want a lawyer!"

The machine beside the bed started beeping. Two nurses and a doctor came into the room.

"Sorry, detectives," the doctor said with scorn, "enough for now."

Mark shut his eyes. All he wanted was to see that Brian was alive—that he was okay.

#

Around 4 o'clock that afternoon, Mark woke up. The same doctor he saw earlier gave him an itemized list of the damage. Miraculously, nothing was broken, but he had some internal damage, and they had to operate. The doctor spewed a string of twelve-letter words Mark had never heard before. The message, however, was clear. Not only was he lucky… but he'll live.

One thing had changed; he woke up wearing a shiny pair of handcuffs—one end attached to his left wrist and the other to the bed. He also noticed the guard posted outside his door.

"Hey Doc, one more thing," Mark said. "I was with a kid. Please tell me...he's okay? I really need to know."

"The boy, Brian?"

Mark nodded.

"He's fine, and he says it's because of you. He's got a broken leg, and we're keeping him for observation. Says you saved his life, and he keeps asking about you. I was told not to tell you." He made a face. "Tweedledum and Tweedledee are barking up the wrong tree, aren't they?"

"More than you know."

"Why won't you help them?"

"I just got out of prison today. We don't quite see eye to eye. They already have the person they believe is responsible, and now they'll probably say there was no other man—that it was just me all along. I blew up the train with me on it so that I would have an alibi or something."

"Yeah, they definitely have their heads up their ass," the doctor said with a chuckle. Then his face tightened. "Here they come, and they have company."

The two detectives entered the room with company. Judging by the appearance of the other three people, they brought Defense and Homeland Security with them. *Now the games will really begin.*

"I already told you I answer no questions until I see a lawyer."

One of the new people stepped forward. A blonde woman pushing 40 with a severe-looking facial expression that said:

I-don't-take-orders-from-nobody-I-give-them: "Well, Mr. Toren, I'm sorry to inform you, you don't have any rights. A domestic terrorist caught in the act, well, just doesn't."

Mark laughed.

A full belly, bouncing bellow. "I'm still not talking," he said in between fits. "For once in my life…I was the good guy, so go fuck yourselves. I still want an attorney. And…I want to see Brian," Mark shouted, determined not to play their games.

Tension filled the room.

The blonde woman turned out to be from homeland security, Agent Angela Rothman. She continued with her threats. Thoughts of waterboarding filled his mind. Detective Franklin and Reynolds added they got him on video at every explosion.

They had it all figured out, and the short version went something like this: somehow, he planned this act of terrorism with an accomplice from his prison cell. Angry that he had been sent away, he hooked up with someone else who was angry at the government and wanted revenge. And this imaginary person sets the plan into action. Of course, this story has huge gaping holes—the big one. What about Mark saving the kid? They had an answer. Simple. Brian was only a convenience; Mark needed to pull someone out to give himself an alibi. *Unfucking believable.*

Eventually, the conspiracy theory crackpots left, leaving Mark to his own thoughts. He tugged on the handcuffs and looked around for something he could use. Mark didn't like being a sitting duck—being cuffed to the bed did exactly that. News of the warehouse explosion survivors had to have been on the news.

Mark picked up the remote and turned on the television. Channels clicked on and off as Mark flipped through the channels to a local news station: *BREAKING NEWS*.

Every news update today seemed to be breaking news. A news anchor, a woman of about 30 with long dark brown hair, recapped the morning's events. The time at the bottom left-hand corner of the screen read 7PM. Had all of this really played out in less than twelve hours? It seemed impossible. Mark's face popped up on the screen, and his involvement was inundated with words such as Person of Interest, Suspected Domestic Terrorist, Long Criminal History, and so on. He had somehow become the scapegoat—*he wasn't a happy camper.*

There was no mention of Brian or the possibility of anyone else. The authorities gave Boston citizens a false sense of security, and Mark hoped nobody would pay for it. They stressed the point that they had a suspect in custody. The anchor remarked how the attacks had stopped since he was taken into custody after nearly blowing himself up.

"Protect the boy, you stupid, ignorant assholes; he's after the fuckin boy!"

He had to get out of these cuffs, he thought, *and get to work.*

Before Mark could get the handcuffs off, the doctor from earlier stepped into the room with the officer.

"I need to take him down the hall for some tests. You're welcome to come along," the doctor said to the officer.

"Well, I guess I have to anyway," he said, unlocking Mark's handcuffs.

"I'm taking him to x-ray, so he can't be wearing those," he said. "And I'm sure he'll be a good boy…won't you, Mark?"

"Sure," Mark said, thinking x-rays? He didn't break anything. Then he remembered Brian had broken his leg.

The police officer checked the x-ray room, which had a door that led to another room. He checked the door, and it was locked. Mark sat on the table while the officer had the doctor unlock the door. The room was being used; a child was getting an x-ray on his leg that was already in a cast. He asked the doctor about it.

"The kid complained of pain, so we wanted to ensure the bones are set right."

The cop seemed to buy what the doctor said because he nodded and left the room.

Mark's only expression was a suppressed smile.

After the cop left, Mark grinned widely. "Why're you taking the risk, Doc?"

"One reason only…Brian is not cooperating. Yes, tests need to be done, and he refuses to do them unless he can see you. When he saw you were being blamed for the attacks on the news, he got hysterical. So for his recovery, I thought it was the best thing to do. Now, if you'll excuse me for a moment."

The doctor walked over to the door and opened it. A moment later, Brian raced into the room. Besides the cast on his leg, he looked okay—the second he saw Mark, he smiled.

"Mark," he said a bit too loudly, then quickly covered his mouth before going over to Mark. Brian hugged Mark tightly, his head resting on Mark's chest. "I told my dad, and he told me he'll try to help you."

Mark smiled. "That's good. I can use all the help I can get right now." He pushed Brian away to look him in the eye. "What's this that I heard about you not doing as you're told?"

Brian's face lost all the brightness it had a moment before. "But I—"

"Save it, I understand, but I know you want to get better—don't you?"

"Yeah," Brian said as a tear rolled down from his right eye. "I just needed to see you, is all? But I promise I'll behave."

"You should never have to promise; you know why?"

Brian shook his head.

"Because your word should always be enough," Mark said. "To paraphrase the Bible, 'your yes should be yes, and your no should be no.' You understand what I'm trying to tell you?"

Brian nodded and hugged Mark again but tighter. "I do. Never say something you don't mean. I prom—" he cut himself off. "My word will always be enough."

"Good." Mark stood up. "Now, are you satisfied that I'm, okay?"

"A-huh"

"Then you should be going. I don't want this nice doctor to get in trouble, do you?"

"No. Can he?"

"Yes, we're not supposed to be seeing each other right now."

"I know. My dad told me," Brian said remorsefully. "But said he'd fix it."

"Well, in that case, I hope he can, now go on and be—"

"Good," Brian said with a smile. "I will."

He disappeared back behind the door from which he came and was gone.

Mark looked at the doctor. "Thank you for everything."

The doctor told him not to worry about it, and they left the x-ray room, and a moment later, he was back in his room.

21

ALIVE

When Parker became conscious, he found himself in complete darkness. He had no idea of his location, and his head and body ached. Parker scrambled to his feet as the fog lifted from his head. He stumbled across the room to the door, stopping at the heavy bag, which still swayed back and forth. After exiting, Parker turned right, went through the maze of the warehouse proper, and out through the exit. Once Parker believed he was a safe distance away, he removed his cellphone and placed the call. He hoped it would be the last call he had to make. The line connected, and he hung up.

A moment later, a brilliant white-hot flash followed by an earth-shattering rumble shook the buildings around him. Debris rained down. He took cover and looked back in the warehouse's direction to check out his handiwork. A huge fireball rose into the sky. Parker smiled, deciding it would be best not to be discovered at the scene. After exiting the alley, they walked two blocks to O'Shea's bar. The neon green sign beckoned him. He took a seat at the bar, ordered a drink, and watched what was on TV, but it wasn't lost on him that a decade or two ago, he would've got flack for doing just that. Soon, the authorities would search the remains of the warehouse.

The bartender, a redheaded fellow named Mickey, placed the drink in front of him before he could say a word. "Did you feel the earth shake? Many people don't realize we get earthquakes. They're mild, so most people don't know,"

"I don't know about all that, Mickey, but I don't think it was a tremor."

"No, what could it be?" Mickey asked with a slight Irish accent.

"I heard a loud thunderous roar like a freight train, and the night sky became awash with light, so you tell me?"

"Another explosion?"

"That's what I believe, but who knows, I don't," Parker said, taking a sip of his beer. "Though the news should tell us something. But you never have the news on."

"True. How very true," Mickey said as he turned and reached up to the TV and changed the station to a local news channel. "It's been on every channel today, but there you go."

Half the screen was filled with capital letters declaring breaking news—images of firefighters battling a terrible blaze behind them. An African-American news anchor appeared with close-cropped hair and a cherubic face.

"The four-alarm fire…behind me…has been burning for 20 minutes. Witnesses say the building just exploded, and as you can see, it has been completely destroyed. Nothing but a pile of burning rubble—"

The news anchor put his right hand to his ear.

"—This just in…there are survivors. Firefighters have just removed two people from the rubble." He turned to look over his shoulder. "And they're being loaded into ambulances as we speak"

The picture cut to two ambulances as an emergency response team wheeled two gurneys to the waiting, open doors. The camera zoomed in. An outline of a man could be clearly seen on the first gurney, but he was quickly loaded into the ambulance. The other, which the camera now zoomed in on, revealed a small figure who appeared to be awake and moving. The camera zoomed in more for a better closeup. Brian's face filled the screen. The boy looked like he was in a great deal of pain. The picture flicked back to the anchor, who babbled on about the blaze and how today was indeed a bad day.

Fuck! Parker screamed inside his head. *Alive!*

Mickey went to change the channel, seeing enough disaster for one day.

"Hey, Mick, leave it on," Parker said. "I think I know that guy."

Mickey shrugged, then moved on to another patron.

Parker needed to know which hospital. As if the news anchor had heard him. "The two survivors will be taken to Tufts Medical Center."

22

BRIAN'S FATHER

"He's my client, and this is a United States court order! Bellowed a deep baritone voice.

Mark turned his head from the television toward the door and wondered who the person was.

"Then call the agent-in-charge—now!" The man's voice ordered. "I want to see my client."

The voice commanded authority.

His client? The man was a lawyer. Was he his? Brian's dad, maybe, he didn't know.

The voice lowered its volume, and the tone became a hushed urgency as another man's voice entered the conversation. Then a woman's. Mark smiled as he stared at the door, wishing he could see through it because it sounded like Agent Rothman had just got a serious tongue lashing. A moment later, there was complete silence, and the door to his room swung open.

A man, perhaps in his midthirties, walked in. He was of average height, with dark brown hair, almost black. His face was narrow with features that looked as if they'd been cast out of bronze, but his bright and penetrating eyes were a beacon of hope.

The man closed the door and approached Mark as he offered his hand. "Hi, I am—"

"I know who you are," Mark smiled. "Your son looks just like you."

"Well, I'll take that as a compliment," he said. "Unfortunately, if you'd seen his mother, you would know where he really got his looks."

Mark smiled. The man before him had an easy honesty about him. He exuded an air of trust—and Mark knew a straight shooter when he saw one.

"So you're my attorney?"

"Yes, if you want me to be?"

"You're obviously expen—"

He held up his hand. "Stop. Money is not the issue. You're getting railroaded because of post-9/11 hysteria combined with the not too long-ago Boston bombings, but if you want to talk money, just answer me this one question. How much is my son's life worth?"

Mark swallowed hard but remained silent.

"Because from the way I see it, I owe you."

"I'm sorry—"

"For what?" Brian's dad smiled. "Forget it. Let's get to work."

Their conversation lasted 20 minutes. Michael, Brian's dad, told Mark what he intended to do and had already filed several motions. He hoped Mark would be released from DHS custody by morning.

"Look, I know you don't trust the government, and I'm not asking you to, but I am asking you to have a little faith in me. I'm good at what I do, so I'm told—and when the government is wrong, they're wrong. This time they're big-time wrong, and I think they know it."

"If they know they're wrong, why haven't they let me go?"

"They have you at the scene of every attack. Brian told them what happened several times, and so far, his story has never changed. That's the good thing about truth; it doesn't change. The thing is, they don't believe this is about Brian." He gathered his thoughts. "It's hard for them to believe someone's doing all this to kill a kid. No, they believe it's got something to do with you."

"Me? He tried to blow up Brian inside your building."

"I know, and he almost succeeded, but you told Brian the guy looked familiar to you."

"He does, and I heard him use my name when he tried to scare Brian out from his hiding place."

"Brian said the same thing, and that's why Agent Rothman believes you're involved somehow."

"So now, what do I do?"

"Just relax, and hopefully, I can get you released before they try to move you."

After a moment of silence, Michael got up from his chair. Mark knew the consultation was now over.

"Are you taking Brian home?"

"No, they're keeping him for observation," he replied, making eye contact. "Why?"

"I don't know why, but he is after Brian."

"I know he is," he said, then sighed heavily. "I only wish I knew the reason myself."

"I've been around the criminal element a long time. Since I was a kid," Mark said. "This guy, he's trying to prove a point. A sadistic one but one nonetheless."

"You think he might try to finish what he started," Michael said, despair filling his voice. "Is that what you're telling me?"

"No…I'm telling you…what he's gonna do."

23

I'M COMING

O' Shea's was packed with regulars who just got off work. Parker still sat at the bar, his vision locked onto the TV— Two hours of uninterrupted newscast. Parker loved seeing Mark's face flashed on the screen as a person of interest, which had been upgraded 30 minutes ago to a potential suspect in the bombings, including the warehouse.

Fresh out of prison, according to reports, this has to be his worst nightmare. Parker smiled despite himself. He looked around the room. The chatter in the pub remained grim since the moment he arrived; the faces in the room were glum. Parker pushed back another smile. That's right, be afraid, be terribly afraid. Any day can be yours, your family, friends, whoever's time to perish.

Parker glanced at his watch—time to go. He stood, paid Mickey, and left the bar. On the street, Parker flagged down a taxi. He got in, and several minutes later, he was standing in front of a three-story brownstone in the south end. Though he technically lived there, he hadn't stepped foot into the house but three times since getting out of prison 16 months prior. He climbed the stairs to the front door and let himself in.

The place held too many memories for him. Most of them were so good they hurt. The last time he "lived" there was with his wife and child—when things were good. Before the cruel world took them away from him: His child… and…his wife. Pictures of a happy family adorned the walls and all available space in every room and along the walls of the three flights of stairs.

Moving through the house, his emotions stirred deep within him. He pushed him back down, so he could concentrate on what he came to get from upstairs. Every good plan has a backup. Although he thought the knapsack filled with disks that he had in his son's bedroom would be used for an entirely different purpose—taking his own life.

He climbed the stairs to the second-floor landing, which contained four bedrooms and a full bathroom. He turned right and walked down the long hallway. Light glinted from a window at the other end. Shadows danced around him.

"Soon, I'll be with you," he said aloud, stopping before the room's door. He took a deep breath and entered the room. The knapsack lay on the bed where he left it—and planned to meet his maker. The pack contained enough explosives to demolish the entire building. Parker, a proud homeowner, loved the old brownstone. Over the years, they restored the old home to its original grandeur.

After sitting on the bed, he opened the pack and removed a bomb vest of his design. The vest had six specially made pockets for the disks to be inserted into with a snug fit, which were positioned to do maximum damage. The vest was made for him, but he might need it for someone else.

He reached back into the back, removed several disks, and placed them into each pocket. He set the vest aside and looked into the pack to see how many disks remained. He took three disks and put the rest back in the bag, and zipped it up. Closed up tight. He swung it over his shoulder as he stood. With the three disks in his left hand, he left the room.

Every structure had weak and strong points. Parker moved through the house, placing the disks in three strategic locations to ensure the most structural damage. Once outside on the sidewalk, he stopped and looked back at the house one more time—taking in the memories of the old building.

He walked a couple of blocks before he hailed a taxi. The ride to the hospital took five minutes. He paid the driver and got out. He stood impatiently before the huge hospital building. Over the years, raising a child brought him to this place…many…many…times. More of those good memories flooded his conscious mind. Anger rose within him, along with a bilious rage. He skulked to the entrance.

The thick gray sky made it seem even darker when night fell. The heavens feeling despair for the tragic bloodshed of the day—once again cried out in protest. Rain pelted the street in heavy torrents of sudden sorrow.

Parker made it to the floor where they had Mark with no issues. Not barely a soul glanced in his direction at all. Though he wasn't surprised to see a cop parked outside Mark's door, he'd hoped there wouldn't be one. They held Brian in a different part of the hospital. He walked down the corridor, passed the guard, and made his way to pediatrics. At the end of the hallway, he could go straight or turn right.

Deciding a distraction on Mark's floor would hopefully put more suspicion on him, he turned right. After another right turn, the third room on the left was empty. He entered the room and realized that the unit he was now in was geriatrics. He shook his head as he thought he was about to do about half of them a favor. He removed the disk from the knapsack, tossed it on the bed, and left.

Several minutes later, he was in pediatrics, standing in front of Brian's hospital room. The door was closed, but not one cop was in sight. He entered the dark room. The boy, curled up in the bed fast asleep, did not feel his presence.

24

NINTH ATTACK HOSPITAL

Mark stared out his window, and an inky, impenetrable blackness stared back at him. He could almost see his own image in the glass. After Brian's father left, Mark tried to take a nap, but he couldn't get comfortable. Brian's father promised them he'd stay with his son. Mark described the man to Brian's father, and Michael told him he'd relay the message to the hospital. It should've squelched his screaming, worrying mind because Michael was the kid's father, for Christ's sake. *It didn't.*

He tossed and turned for about a quarter of an hour, which seemed like forever. Not an easy task to begin with when being shackled to a bedpost. He repositioned himself once more and stared at the ceiling for a couple of minutes before gazing deeply into the abyss beyond the window, knowing the man was out there. Knowing he would come—and probably already had.

However, there was one thing Mark could do: grasp onto the cuff and pull with the strength of a dozen warriors. Nothing. DHS already named Mark their suspect, so he could hope the man decided not to show his face and just let Mark take the fall, but that was stuff created especially for fiction—not real life.

Years surrounded by the worst humankind had to offer had opened his eyes, and his experience told him that the man wouldn't stop. He had a mission any point to prove—and it had yet to be completed. Mark sat up, swung his legs over the side, and tore at the rubbery plastic bracelet on his non-shackled wrist until it came free.

It took him a while, but he managed to tear a strip thin enough for him to slide it into the cuff. He then pressed the arms together, tightening it until it clicked twice. He winced in pain as he pushed the strip under the metal arm. Another click. He tried it again, and nothing. No click. He pulled the arm, and the bracelet came free. He grabbed his wrist, massaging it with his other hand. With his hand now free, he collapsed back onto the pillow and shut his eyes—and sleep snatched him away.

###

A loud noise rousted Mark from his sleep. He sat up with a start. A flash of light crackled outside, illuminating the window with bright light. Is there a thunderstorm? He wiped the sleep from his eyes before padding over to the window. Behind him, he heard a commotion in the hallway.

The lightning probably gave some poor soul a heart attack, he thought, as he waited for another flash. He didn't see any rain. Immediately, he knew something was wrong.

Red and orange flames licked the black sky. The blackness hungrily devoured the flame.

He went to the door and pulled it open just enough to see beyond its confines. People were scrambling in every direction. He opened the door further and peered out in both directions. The officer was gone—and nobody seemed to notice him. Mark merged with a crowd headed toward the section that was ablaze. He made it to the wing in a short time, but he'd been in such a state, that he'd forgotten to get dressed.

He read the nameplates of each room he passed. Nick Mitchell read the third plate. He stepped inside the room, and as he expected, it was empty. He looked around for clothes. Something to wear. Anything at this point besides the hospital johnny and his underwear would do. *Please have been in as much of a rush as he was.*

He checked the closet and found jeans, a black T-shirt, and a pair of Adidas, a size too small. Mark put on the street clothes.

Once he was dressed, he ran toward the fire.

The wing was ablaze. He had no idea where Brian's room was but assumed the fire was in that direction. He continued onward to pediatrics but still panicked. His heart dropped to the pit of his stomach as worry, dread, and grief tried to take control. He shook it off as he glanced around. "Wait a minute. This isn't pediatrics," he said aloud to nobody in particular.

Mark looked back the way he came and saw a sign hanging from the ceiling: Pediatrics with an arrow pointing toward the other wing. He whipped his head back toward the fire. He paused for a moment, unsure what to do, but his intuition was never wrong.

A Distraction.

He ran back the way he came, following the signs to pediatrics. The hallway that led to the unit stretched like the entire length of a football field but probably wasn't. Mark picked up speed, made it to the doors, and rushed through. He found a dead calm. Silence. The fire alarms were not going off in this part of the building. Mark could see the other end of the unit. Doctors and nurses milled about. A security officer glanced at him suspiciously, but the guard stopped to talk to a nurse at the nurses' station. *That's right, player. Do your thing and get that number—and pay no attention to me.*

Mark walked five feet and stopped dead in his tracks with his mouth agape. At the other end of the corridor stood a man grinning. The person who caused all this madness. He blinked. Anger welled up inside him as he stepped closer. The man smiled and made a slicing gesture across his throat and smiled again just before disappearing through a door behind him. One marked exit.

Mark went in the direction the man had come from. He knew Brian's room had to be that way. He looked into each room he passed as he read each nameplate—

He saw a person lying motionless on the floor before he could read the nameplate and stepped into the room. Michael moved with an audible moan.

Mark immediately glanced at Brian, who sat on his bed with a look of terror. In each hand, he held something silver. A cord snaked down from each cylinder, disappearing into the folds of his blanket. Terror screamed inside Mark's mind. *No, no, no. Please, no.* "Don't move or let them go," he warned, stepping closer to the bed. "Let me see where those wires go, okay?"

Silent tears rolled down Brian's cheeks.

Mark's heart went out to the kid. He glanced back at Brian's father, who was now fully conscious and groaning in pain. He looked up at Mark. Eyes wide and pleading.

"You might want to leave the room," Mark said.

"No," he said to Mark. "If he's holding what I think it is, then we're all in this together" Michael slowly got to his feet.

Time to focus.

Mark turned back to Brian, reached for the edge of the blanket, and pulled it slowly off him. Brian managed to stay still, although he was shaking. Afraid. Mark took a deep breath when he saw the device—a pressure plate.

The plate was made entirely out of some kind of hard plastic. It was approximately 2 1/2 feet squared. No wires other than the two that led from the two cylinders Brian held in each hand. *Was that the backup?*

"Did he say anything to you?" Mark asked Brian.

Brian nodded and glanced worriedly at his father.

"What did…he…tell…you? Mark asked slowly. More tears flowed. Brian's eyes glistened. "It's okay. I know you're scared. I haven't lied to you yet—have I?"

He shook his head.

"Nor am I about to. Most likely, we're all going to get blown to shit. But if there's a chance to save you, it will all be worth it. I'm glad I got a chance to meet you" Brian smiled at the remark. "But neither of us wants that to happen, do we?"

Again the shake of the head. "No," he said, barely audible.

"Well, I need you to be brave, strong, yet scared to hell enough to tell me what he told you. It might be helpful."

Mark glanced over at Brian's father, who was now standing on the opposite side of the bed.

"Like I said, Bri," Michael said, swallowing hard, and placed his hand on Brian's shoulder. "We're in this together."

Brian looked at both men and took a deep breath. "The man told me if I didn't hold these things," holding up the two cylinders, "I'd blow to pieces…." He sobbed lightly. "He also said that I had to sit just the way I am."

Mark nodded, getting the message.

He looked at his father, then quickly back to Mark. "He also told me it was…um…uh…my…dad's…fault." Brian stopped and took a deep breath. "Then he said…'he was… sorry…that his loss will be my father's.'"

Brian's father squeezed his son's shoulder but looked at Mark. "What do you think we should do?"

Having no idea what they should do, he shrugged at a loss. "I don't know. Get help, I suppose."

"You should go," Michael said. "Brian's my son."

Mark stopped at the door; something about what Brian told him bothered him. He stopped as the words flashed across his mind—*'his loss will be my father's.'* Something clicked inside his head. He turned back and looked at Brian's father. "Do you have your cellphone on you?"

"Yes, of course," he said, stuffing his hand into his coat pocket. "It's right—"

He cut himself off. His face turned ashen.

"What's the matter?"

Michael removed his hand, but what he held wasn't his cellphone, but a rectangular-shaped piece of plastic about the size of Brian's father's iPhone. "What is this?"

Mark cursed himself. "I don't—I'm sorry, I think I just fucked up. Did you feel anything slide into place when you grabbed hold of it?"

"Yeah, I think I did."

"It's as he told Brian. You'll suffer as he does. The man doesn't want to kill you. No. He wants you to live, grieve, and feel what he feels."

A strange wave of tension contorted Brian's father's face. Then a look Mark could only describe as one of understanding. Recognition, but to whatever that may have been, Mark had no idea.

"You all right?" Mark said, reaching over.

"Yeah, I was just thinking about something. Now…what were you saying? I kinda zoned out for a moment, so continue."

"Well, if I'm right—"

Something was still off.

"—as long as you stay near Brian, nothing can happen."

"His face contorted with understanding. "Because if I die, then I can't suffer."

"You got it."

Both men looked at Brian. Still, there was something—

And it was his father who noticed what the something was. "When did you get dressed?" he asked Brian.

Mark didn't notice what was in plain sight because he focused on the bomb, not Brian. *How obvious*, Mark thought now. Brian was fully clothed in sweatpants and a sweatshirt. He could even see the color of a T-shirt underneath.

Brian looked down at himself and cleared it up for them into two words. "Not me," he said, his voice quivering slightly.

Mark couldn't blame the kid for being scared. At first, he thought a bomb was underneath him, but the mechanism was just a prop if what Mark now believed was correct. The man expected Brian's father to freak out and run for help. The guy played on the heartstrings of a father, and with Mark running to a wild goose chase of a fire, it might've worked. If he hadn't realized he was headed away from Brian, he would've been consoling Brian's father at this moment for the loss of his son. *Clever son of a bitch.*

"Lift your shirt," he said in a cautious tone, "slowly."

Fear spread across Brian's face, but he obeyed, lifting his shirt to reveal what reminded Mark of a bulletproof vest. Though Mark was positive what was under the cloth material would not save your life but take it.

Mark nodded toward Brian, letting Brian know he could stop. Then he took a deep breath as he reached out with both arms.

"No, I'll do it," Michael said.

"You can't," Mark said flatly. "If you release that device, we're all dead."

Brian's father told him to go to Mark.

"You sure I won't explode," Brian said, tears flowing from his eyes as they streamed down his face.

"As sure as I can be."

Still looking unsure, Brian reached out to Mark, and he swept Brian into his arms.

Nothing.

Whew, that was close—

The bed lit up in a small blast, enough to engulf the bed but no more. Nonetheless, he and Brian fell back. Mark felt the front of him become wet.

"Sorry," Brian whispered into Mark's ear.

"Don't worry about it, Lil man," Mark said as he locked eyes with Brian. "I think I wet myself too… Let's get out of here and make sure we stay close."

They left the room…and…stopped dead in their tracks.

25

BOMB SQUAD

"Freeze!" An agent shouted.

At least half a dozen agents aimed assault weapons at them and moved toward them from where Mark had come. He glanced at the exit. The agent stepped closer.

"Put down the kid and put your hands up. Now!"

Mark stared at them; a deer caught in headlights.

"The other one has something in his hand," one of them shouted.

"A weapon," another interjected.

Like hungry, angry insects, red dots swarmed over Brian's father's chest. Mark stepped in front of Michael. The angry red swarm now danced across Brian's back.

"Drop that weapon and put that kid down. Now."

The situation could not have gotten any worse. Mark didn't like it one bit. He didn't trust cops of any kind, not just because he was a criminal but because cops, albeit crooked, did most of the dirtiest shit he'd ever seen.

Many of them, he was sure, were just doing their jobs, but they were terrible at reading people. Cops on television could always read the situation. In reality, innocent people were shot or even dead because of their ineptitude. Criminals were better trained than most cops.

"He's the kid's father, and he can't—"

"Drop the weapon. Your last warning and get on the floor," the leader commanded.

Why hadn't they already fired on him? You'd be mistaken if you believe cops wouldn't shoot somebody when there was a high chance of injuring or possibly killing some kid.

The bombs.

They're afraid Mark may have an explosive device. Well, they were wrong—sorta. But I'm sure they didn't expect it to be Brian.

"That's a trigger in his hand…and he can't put it down," Mark shouted.

The approaching agents stopped…then stepped back.

That's right.

Mark scanned the agents' faces. No signs of Detective Franklin or Reynolds—or the DHS woman. The DHS Agent in Charge approached from behind the agents with her gun drawn. She made her way to the front of the pack.

"Don't shoot. Don't shoot." She called. "Stand down."

Their weapons lowered.

About time someone with some sense, so he hoped.

"Mark…put the kid down," she said, "and we'll talk."

"There's nothing to talk about," he said and immediately regretted how that sounded.

The guns came back up this time without the dancing ants.

"Stand down," she said, almost angry. "I said…stand down."

Reluctantly, they complied.

"W–we need bomb squad," Mark said. "If Michael puts down that device, we'll all blow the fuck up, so that ain't gonna happen. We told you the kid was in trouble, and the man was after him, but you didn't listen, so now we're here."

"I'm listening now," she said.

"Then get someone from the bomb squad, now!"

She turned to one of the agents and nodded. They talked into the mic. "They're on the way."

"You satisfied?"

"For now," he said, adjusting his grip on Brian.

"All right, now put the kid down and let him come to us."

Brian hugged Mark tighter as he emphatically shook his head. "No, don't. I don't wanna get down. They'll shoot you if I do," Brian cried.

"Sorry…you heard him…I can't."

"And why not?"

Mark tried to avoid answering for the kid's sake. "Where do you think the bomb is located? Do you fuckin understand now why we need the bomb squad?"

The agent's face turned ashen. She turned to the same agent.

"I'm already on it," he said.

She turned back to Mark. "Can I approach?"

"Why couldn't you? Of course, you can," he said, his anger rising. "I told you I have nothing to do with this—nothing, so come on and see for yourself."

Agent Rothman approached them slow and steady. She approached. Mark motioned for her to check Brian for herself. She lifted his shirt and then patted Brian on his head. "It's going to be all right. You'll need to be brave for a little longer."

"The man tried to trick us. That device was in his pocket; we thought it was his cellphone. The man knew Brian's father would panic when he saw Brian sitting on a pressure plate, holding two cylinders in each hand, and run to get help. Inadvertently—"

"Blowing me up," Brian said in a low, somber tone.

"You're really not involved, are you?"

Brian summed it up best. "Duh."

Mark suppressed a laugh. "Never mind that right now; we need to get this off him."

"All right," she conceded, getting the message. "They should be here any moment." Agent Rothman turned back to the other agents. "All right, team, set up a perimeter. Nobody gets inside this ward unless I say so, got it?"

"Yes, ma'am," they said before doing what they were told.

"And someone put out that damn fire," she ordered, pointing toward Brian's room, engulfed in flames. She looked up at Mark. "That's weird; I wonder why the sprinklers didn't come on?"

"I don't know," he said as he saw two men in full bomb gear come onto the ward. "They're here'"

"Good," she said and left to greet the bomb squad.

"I think it's safe now, Brian," Mark said. "Do you want to get down?"

"Brian shook his head. "Nah, not really," he said, "unless you're tired."

"I like to say I'm not, but you ain't exactly light, and I think my Staples just opened."

"Put me down. Put me down," Brian commanded. "I didn't know I was hurting you."

When Agent Rothman returned with the two bomb squad techs, he put Brian down.

"Lift your shirt to show them?" Agent Rothman asked.

Brian nodded.

The woman spoke first. "We'll need to remove that shirt, okay."

Brian started taking off—

"No, stop," she said, suddenly holding up a pair of scissors. "We'll cut it off to be on the safe side."

"Okay," Brian said, his voice barely audible.

A moment later, Brian's shirt lay in tatters on the floor. Seeing the bomb strapped to his chest made Mark fantasize about doing seriously nasty torture to the man when he found him. *He better hope that the agents find him first*, he thought as he watched the bomb experts do their job. While she looked at Brian's bomb, her partner examined the metal device Brian's father clutched in a death grip.

Brian's father had been quiet for a long time, and Mark hoped the man was all right. Though he was certain, seeing a bomb strapped to his son's chest invoked similar thoughts as his own, if not worse. Despite everything, Mark thought Michael was holding up well.

Twenty minutes passed by as if a snail carried time on its back. The bomb technician worked with a precise hand to determine whether she could remove the device without making it go off. The vest was made out of Kevlar. The technician cut out a three-inch square between Brian's chest and abdominal area to see what they were dealing with. The plastic explosive material had been spread in a single layer between the vest's front and back shell. Although lightweight, it was a bullet-proof vest.

It took 18 minutes to find the control device and deviate the connection to remove the vest. With a methodical hand, she slowly lifted the vest. Brian shook nervously in a state of panic. Mark stepped toward him.

"It's alright, Lil man, we'll do this together."

"That's right, son," Brian's dad agreed. "Together."

"I'm going to help you remove the vest...if that's okay?" Mark asked the bomb tech.

"No, that's fine. The minute you came over, he stopped shaking."

"Let's do it."

Brian stood with his arm straight up over his head. Beads of sweat streaked down his face, along with silent sobbing. The vest was too tight to lift over Brian's head, so they had to undo several straps secured by a plastic latch like on a backpack.

"I already checked each strap and didn't see any wires or other foreign objects, but I want you to check yours and then double-check mine."

"Okay," Mark said. "Am I gonna loosen the straps or undo them completely?"

"If we're sure there are no wires, we'll unclasp them."

Mark nodded as he sucked in a deep breath. "I don't see any."

"Okay, good," the tech said. "I don't either. Are you ready?"

"As I'll ever be."

The woman nodded toward Brian.

Mark got the message. "Are you ready?"

Brian opened his mouth, choked on the words, and took a deep breath, following Mark's example. "Think so. Are they gonna make any noise? Because if they snap or something—I think I'll jump out my sneakers."

Not the time to do the talking thing, Mark thought as he looked at the bomb tech.

The tech cracked a smile and shrugged. "They might make a noise, so try to stay in your kicks, alright?"

Brian swallowed a hard, burning lump down his throat. "I'll try."

Mark nodded to the tech, and they unclasped the first one together. Nothing. More sweat rolled down Brian's forehead. Mark's chest tightened as he undid the last one. He looked back to the tech, who nodded.

"All right, Brian, we're gonna lift it over your head now. The side flaps are now open, so you can put down your arms."

"Good, I was getting tired," Brian said with a nervous laugh.

They raised the vest partially over Brian's head, just high enough for Brian to step away.

"Go over to Agent Rothman," Mark said.

Brian looked up at Mark, then at his father, and back to Mark. "I'm sure," Mark said.

Brian went to where Agent Rothman stood.

They lowered the vest to the ground. The bomb tech's partner wheeled over a metal container that looked several inches thick.

"You don't have to help anymore," the tech said. "My partner will do it."

"I've gone this far."

Brian's father stood there nervously because he still held the proximity detonator.

Her partner opened the hatch on the bomb containment apparatus.

"All right, we'll pick it up and put it inside. I don't need to tell you we must be careful now, do I?"

"No, not really," Mark said, "but I thought plastic explosives were stable."

"They are, but we don't know if there are any triggers besides the ones he's holding."

Mark believed they would've already gone off if there were extra triggers.

As if reading his mind, the tech said. "We could have missed something."

Mark took another deep breath and squatted down. As he did, the tech carefully got the vest into the container.

Mark let out a breath he didn't know he was holding.

The tech stood and gestured to those around her. "All right, now all of us will go over to the nurses' station. Let's go."

Mark looked at the tech. "Shouldn't we close the hatch?"

"When everyone is a safe distance away, my partner and I will do it. We know the device he's holding is a pressure and proximity trigger. When we cut the connection by closing the hatch, the bomb could go off before it's secure. Takes timing. We need full concentration, so we need everyone to move away far enough for us to concentrate."

They walked down the hall to the Nurse's Station while the two techs sealed the hatch.

Nothing.

Mark looked at Brian's father, who looked nervous.

"You okay?"

"It just started beeping and vibrating."

Mark relayed the info to the bomb techs bringing up the rear.

"Run faster!" The female tech yelled.

A muffled whump whump sound filled the room. Mark turned back in time to see the containment container launch straight into the air, crashing into the ceiling. Then back down, embedding itself into the tiled floor from which it came. Debris from the ceiling rained down upon it. A cloud of dust billowed into the air.

A moment later, the dust settled.

They could now breathe a little easier. Mark glanced around, surveying those around him. Agent Rothman, Brian's father, two bomb techs, and especially Brian. Except for the two techs, Mark could read their facial expressions loud and clear—he's still out there.

26

SEE THE LIGHT

Parker entered the darkened room and made it five feet before noticing the dark form of a man sleeping in a chair beside the bed. He stepped closer. In the dim light, he recognized the man and thought it could not have worked out any better—an impish grin spread across his face. Rain pounded against the window of the otherwise quiet room. He removed the knapsack, opened the front compartment, and removed a small plastic squeeze bottle containing a colorless liquid. Chloroform. Initially, he was going to use it to knock himself out after activating the charges in the vest. He planned to use the chloroform as a backup, so he couldn't back out.

He squirted a small amount of chloroform onto the cloth and approached Brian's father. Michael woke up as Parker approached and stood up in an outright panic. Parker wrestled him quietly to the floor. It was good that Parker had the advantage of size because he had enough trouble as it was. He glanced over at Brian, who was still sleeping. He then checked Brian's father's pockets for anything useful. He found an iPhone, which he hoped to find. He slipped it into his pocket while retrieving a flat metallic object that matched an iPhone's feel and weight. But a smartphone it wasn't. No. The pressure release and proximity trigger was Parker's own design. One of many designs he put to paper while doing time in prison. He bent down and slipped the trigger into the same pocket the cellphone previously occupied. He moved over to the bed...and...Brian.

Brian barely moved when Parker applied the chloroform-soaked rag over his mouth and nose. With Brian out cold, he set the scene like some bizarro movie director.

First, he went to the room's closet, which he found empty. He closed the door and turned around as he scanned the room from right to left. A small blue duffel bag sat between the chair and the bed by the left side of where Brian's father sat. Parker somehow missed it earlier, and it wasn't like he wasn't looking for it then. He crossed the room to the bag, picked it up, and looked inside.

The bag contained exactly what he hoped to find. Clothes. He removed a brand-new sweatsuit, T-shirts, and socks. There was a package of underwear, but he hoped the boy wouldn't need them. Nobody would go au natural under a Johnny, especially a young child. He said, placing the fresh clothes on the bed.

A commotion in the hall made Parker stop. He listened for a moment as a herd of patients, nurses, doctors, and orderlies ran past the room. When the hall fell silent, he turned back to Brian. Parker picked up the knapsack and set it on the bed. He removed its contents: a bomb vest, a flat plastic pad, and two cylindric devices with long cords and set it all on the bed. After setting up the pressure plate, he prepared Brian for his part in the final act.

He stripped Brian of the Johnny, and Parker redressed him. Brian wore just a pair of boxer briefs under the johnny. Parker put a fresh T-shirt on him and placed the vest over it. Once the vest was secured in place, he put another T-shirt over the vest, followed by a sweatshirt and sweatpants.

He moved Brian onto the plate and placed two cylinders in each hand. He smiled at his plan for revenge and the pain he would cause Brian's father. In the end, it would be much more devastating than blowing Brian up on a train. It's going to work. He could feel it deep in his bones. He stepped back and took in his work, and smiled.

Brian stirred a little, so he removed two ammonia capsules from his pocket and broke them open under his nose— Brian's eyes went wide as he became fully conscious but confused. Parker looked over at Brian's dad, who was still unconscious. Brian stared at Parker without emotion…. The chloroform was still having some effect. A moment later, full recognition registered on Brian's face as fear rippled through his body.

He opened his mouth to scream.

Parker grabbed Brian's wrist before he dropped the triggers in fright. "You're not gonna want to do…that!" Parker said, shifting his gaze down to the devices in each hand. Brian looked down. "You drop or let go of either of these," he shook Brian's hand. "You'll blow up into a million little pieces, you understand?"

Brian nodded slightly but couldn't help to fidget a little.

Parker shook his head. "You're not gonna want to move, either. The pad you're sitting on is pressure sensitive; if you move from it, it will explode. So stay just the way you are, got it?"

Tears rolled down Brian's face. However, he tried not to but couldn't help bawling quietly to himself. Parker took compassion for the boy and thought about not going through with the plan. No matter how precious he thought the boy's life was, he knew it needed to be done. *The boy had to die.* Parker removed his cellphone, pressed the preset speed dial number, and glanced at the unconscious man on the floor.

"And I'm sorry…but I'm sure you don't believe me," Parker said, his eyes glistening. "Nevertheless, I am sorry. I know this might be hard for you to understand, but this whole thing has nothing at all to do with you."

Brian wiped his eyes and saw his dad lying on the floor for the first time.

"My dad!" He said with a gasp. "He's not."

"No, he's not," Parker said with a sniff. "Truthfully, I'd rather kill him than you."

"My dad? Why?"

"Because this is all his fault, you must die. He has to feel my pain and my loss. He helped the creep who murdered my child get away with it—"

People rushed past Brian's room. The fires began to blaze. Time to go.

Parker turned from the bed as a tear rolled down his face. He wiped it away, turned back, snatched the empty knapsack off the bed, and headed for the door. He glanced back at Brian, who was bawling with his head in his arms. Parker could see the boy's face contort into complete and utter horror, and it broke his heart, but it had to be done.

Parker had found an excellent location to watch Brian's window from the street. On the way down, he saw Mark but was sure there was nothing he could do to interfere this time. Patiently, he waited for Brian's father to become conscious and see his son in such terror. He had loved to witness the grief that would spread across the man's face when he saw the pressure plate in the detonators in each hand.

He was sure that Michael would run without to get help or maybe use the cellphone—either way, he would inadvertently kill his own son. The anguish will torture Michael for the rest of his life.

Parker believed Michael to be greedy and only out to make money. The end would come by his own hand because of his wrongdoing. Because Michael decided greed was better than justice for his son. Parker could almost taste the acrid smell of blood. Oh, Michael will die, but it will be a slow and treacherous death.

The night sky became black, and there was a chill. The muted city noises were suddenly pierced with sirens—fire and police. If things were to go his way, Mark would take the fall. The news had already painted a nasty picture of his alleged involvement.

Brian's room remained dark.

Moments later, fire trucks arrived, followed by police cars. The police roped off the area around the hospital. As they should, but a bit too late.

Time crawled along.

A flash of light popped behind the window.

He could almost hear the pop to go with it. When no explosion followed, Parker assumed they took a chance, and the boy and father were still together. Michael didn't run to get help but instead tried to save his son's life.

Commendable.

A bright white-hot light flashed through the ward's windows, and the building shook. It wasn't how he imagined it, but he got to witness the explosion go off. He smiled to himself once more.

Time to find a TV and watch it unfold. The end was in sight. However, he had to know for sure they were dead. And he needed to decide whether to kill Mark or let him live. But he'd think more about that later. Now he needed to find a place to watch the news.

27

BRIAN'S FATHER'S OFFICE

The father's office was on the 17th floor and was located in the high-powered law firm of Schmidt, Lauren, and Phillips. Brian's father sat behind a big oak desk. Mark occupied one of the two chairs in front of the desk, and Agent Rothman took up the other. Brian lay on the couch against the wall where he had fallen asleep.

The TV held their attention as if bewitched by a magical being. The TV was in a hidden compartment within a credenza when it wasn't in use.

BREAKING NEWS flashed across the screen. The news anchor appeared and read the update on the latest explosion. "The attacks claimed five more lives and injured 27 others in the ninth attack. This last attack was at a hospital in Chinatown. The authorities were flummoxed by how the attacker escaped from his hospital room and set fire to a section of the hospital before finishing what authorities said he had set out to do. During a standoff with police, the man blew himself up along with another man and his son...."

The report went on.

"Do you really think it will work?" Michael said.

"I'm a little confused myself," Mark said. "Shouldn't we be trying to draw him out?"

"We are," Agent Rothman said.

Confused, both men stared at Agent Rothman.

A smile played on her face. "He believes you're dead. He'll relax and hopefully settle back into his normal routine."

"If he does, we'll never find him," Michael said perturbed.

"Wait...a minute...there has to be something Michael and I are missing?

"Back at the hospital, when both of you," indicating to Mark and Brian, "recounted the day's events, your stories only had one difference because—"

"I saw him...on the platform, on the bus, and at Park Station."

"Don't forget the trash receptacle, the old stock exchange, or the bike carrier. You also said you saw him on the news in the crowd."

"You're getting the footage, and that's why...." He pointed to the TV. "We're—"

"Dead," Agent Rothman finished for him.

"When will Mark be able to view the footage?" Michael asked.

"Once it's compiled, it will be sent to me."

"All right," Michael said. "So, I guess we'll be here a while then."

"I assume so," she said, "but sometimes the tech guys can surprise even me."

"Good," Michael said as he stood and crossed over to the right side of the office to a closet. He removed blue jeans and a button-down shirt from a Saks Fifth Avenue Men's Shop bag. He took the goods back over to the desk and set the bag down next to the desk before handing Mark the blue jeans and button-up. "They should fit. The pants are 38/32, and the shirts are double XL."

"Thanks, anything is better than what I'm wearing right now," he said with a sniff. "…I smell like a dead yak."

"Ah, that's what that smell is," Michael said with a laugh. "There's a shower in the bathroom. Through that door." He pointed to a door in the left-hand corner of the room next to a row of windows that lined the wall behind the desk.

Mark went to the bathroom to wash up and change clothes.

# # #

He didn't take long in the shower, but he hoped the footage had arrived. He stepped out of the shower, rinsed off, and put on the new set of clothes. He was glad he somehow made it through this depressing day. The tragedy of the day will haunt his memories for years to come. Mark couldn't relax just yet. Not until the man was stopped for good.

After getting dressed, he stepped in front of a body-length fog-free mirror that hung on the back of the door. He appraised his appearance—a little beat-up but looking like a million bucks. The clothes fit as if they were made especially for him. By the feel of the material, he could tell the garments were not cheap. Top-of-the-line. It amazed him how good clothes could make one feel, even though it was purely superficial.

Feeling like a new man, Mark stepped back into the office. As he did, Brian breezed by him, muttering something about it being his turn, and disappeared into the bathroom. The door closed behind him.

Mark smiled. "I see sleeping beauty woke up? Why is he so happy?"

"I told Brian once we're allowed," motioning toward Agent Rothman, "that the four of us would go to his favorite restaurant for dinner." Noticing Mark checking his watch, he added. "Albeit a late dinner."

"Sounds good," Mark said, then turned to Agent Rothman. "Has the footage arrived?"

Mark hadn't noticed until that moment that Agent Rothman was working. Keys clacking on the laptop—basically answering his question.

"Yeah, all the footage we could get on such short notice is here."

Short notice, Mark thought, then decided to let it go. It should have been requested at the very least after the third incident, not in a rush effort after the ninth.

"I'm ready when you are," Mark said.

"Just a second," Agent Rothman said. I'll be done in a moment. I decided to use the time you were washing up in the bathroom to get some paperwork done." A rush of clickety clacks, then silence. "Done."

Mark sat in the chair he'd sat in earlier. Agent Rothman placed the laptop on Michael's desk, and he rolled his chair around to see the screen.

"Now, where was it you first saw him?" Agent Rothman asked.

"On the train, but he was on the platform at Back Bay when we left the station right before the first explosion."

She worked the keys. "An underground train station appeared on the screen. "There are several cameras. Where did you see him"?"

"Oh, on the platform, near the tunnel."

More key clacking and a new image.

A light-skinned man stood in a crystal clear image of that part of the platform—the man.

"Can you zoom in?"

She could and did.

"Is he black?" Michael asked.

"Yes," Mark said.

Agent Rothman captured the man's face and blew it up as large as the program would allow.

"He knows me, but I don't know him," Mark said.

"Mark, you remember what Brian told us," Michael said, "about suffering as he had?"

"Yeah," Mark said, looking at him. "What about it? You know him?"

"That's the thing. That's not who I thought I would see."

"Who did you think you would see?" Agent Rothman asked. "And you're sure it's not him?"

"As sure as I can be," Michael said. First, I thought it had something to do with a client I had ten or eleven years ago. Hold on." He picked up the telephone, asked his secretary for a file, and hung up. "That guy isn't only 100 pounds lighter. He looks black. My client was white. Irish descent, I believe."

"White, so it's not him then," Agent Rothman said.

"It can't be, right," Michael said. "We can't change our skin color."

"I don't know, maybe?" Agent Rothman said.

"Not permanently," Mark said. "But apparently, neither of you've seen that reality show that Ice Cube produced years ago. It was around 2005 or something. He took white and black folks and turned them the opposite color."

"How?" Agent Rothman said.

"Airbrush makeup."

"Let me try something," Agent Rothman said as the keys clicked furiously again.

The secretary came in and handed the files, several of them, to Michael and left.

"My client is dead, so I don't feel that statues apply any-more, so you can look at this file, but I warn you it's not for the weak-hearted."

Mark opened the first file and grimaced at the pictures he found. Most of the photos were of a child badly burned and missing limbs. It was sadly grotesque. Mark didn't need to know what happened to this poor kid. It had been an explosion. Of this, he was certain. He also felt they were on the right track. Mark knew a thing or two about payback, and if that were his kid, he'd want some as well. He looked up at Michael with sadness in his eyes.

"I told you gruesome stuff."

Agent Rothman was unaware of their conversation as she concentrated on her task.

"You got him off, didn't you."

"I did…the sad part is the guy really didn't do it, but Mr. Parker, that's the child's father, would *not* listen."

"Where is the real killer now?"

"Dead. The guy liked to make bombs."

"He blew himself up?" Mark asked, confused.

"Yes, he liked to make bombs that Uncle Sam taught him to do," Michael said. "It was also his job as an explosive demolition expert. Above and on the water. He was talented but had other problems that impaired his skill."

"What happened to the guy you got off?"

"He's dead too?"

"What are you saying?" Mark asked as he found a picture of a boy, perhaps twelve, standing next to a man, who obviously was his father. The man smiled proudly. He knew that smile—a tingling sensation spread out from his gut, spiraling in all directions. He knew the man and the answer. "The father killed him."

"There, I'm done." Agent Rothman said.

Brian came out of the bathroom, looking spick-and-span with his hair standing straight up.

"Hey, Lil man," Mark said with a laugh. "You may want to brush your hair."

"I did," he said incredulously.

"Then you might want to do it again," added his father.

Mark looked at Agent Rothman as Brian went back into the bathroom. "What were you going anyhow?"

"This," she said, turning the screen so the two men could see it. On the screen, the security footage was no longer one of a black man but that of a pasty white guy.

Mark looked at the picture in his hand. "The skin tones off," holding up the picture, "but I know him."

"Now, what do we do?" Michael said.

"She's gonna have him picked up," Mark said.

She nodded. "That's the plan," she said as she picked up the phone. "What's his name?"

It was Michael who told her. "Jonathan Parker."

Brian came back out of the bathroom, his hair fixed in place and with an impish smile. "When can we go eat?" he asked, his smile getting wider. "I'm starving...like Marvin, whoever he is."

Mark laughed.

They all laughed.

Except for Brian, that is.

28

RESTAURANT

Mark expected something like McDonald's or Wendy's, Brian's other favorite restaurants. Instead, he found himself in what he believed to be an exclusive restaurant where chicken fingers would cost $100. The linen-covered tables with matching napkins screamed expensive. Nothing on the menu, not even the appetizers, was under $30; the entrées were well over $100. Mark liked to eat out, but he had never been to a place like this.

Brian's favorite item on the menu, which he wanted Mark to try, was fried ice cream made the way it's made in Mexico, not the Americanized premade version. Mark had never tried fried ice cream before though he had heard of it.

He told Brian he would try it, but first, they had to get through the meal. He just hoped he had room at the end of the dinner, but fancy places were known for small plates. A male server came over and took their order.

The dining room was packed, though it was after 9 o'clock. The place was too nice. The nicest restaurant Mark had ever gone to was probably the 99 restaurant or the Longhorn Steakhouse. Even that was pushing it. He lived on pizza and subs. He talked to Michael and learned a lot about Brian and his father.

Michael was a senior partner at the firm and one of the best defense attorneys in the country. He also learned about their personal life. Mark used to care only about himself but found himself listening and wanting to know more about his new friends. At least he hoped they wanted to be friends.

Brian's mother, Tonya, had died of cancer the year before and had been tough going since, especially for Brian. At least, this was what he got from the conversation. Brian was close to his mom. Although Michael had never actually said it in so many words, he heard it loud and clear. He did, however, praise his son every chance he got. Every ounce, a genuine, proud father. *Why shouldn't he be?* Brian was a good kid.

Not having any children—Mark's only regret.

They had been at the restaurant for almost an hour, and not once had the day's events come up. For this, he was grateful. But it still weighed heavily on his shoulders. He could understand the kid surviving, but him? He'd question anyone's God for making that decision. Mark believed he should have been among the dozens of people who died for no other reason than his sordid past. He questioned why he, of all people, was spared. Redemption? Maybe that's what this is. I'm finally earning my keep…about time."

"So, what are your plans?" Michael asked. "Now that you're out, I mean."

"Well, truthfully, I don't know," he said, a bit pensive. "Find a place to live, I suppose. I'll probably rent a room somewhere—and I need to find a job. That might be a bit difficult with how things are right now, but I will if I have to work for minimum wage. I won't like it, but sometimes you have to do what you don't like…to get by. Legitimately, I should add."

"I can agree with that," Michael said, glancing over at his son. "I believe our sacrifices are what makes us." He nodded toward Brian, drawing in a sketchpad he had brought from his dad's office. "Whatever you decide, you seem like a man determined to start over, and I hope you find whatever it is you're looking for."

"Redemption."

"What?" Michael said with a smile, wiping his mouth with his napkin. "What did you say…redemption?"

"It's what I'm searching for. I did a lot of wrong throughout my life and caused many problems and a shit ton of grief. And I believe we end up where we need to be. No matter how good or bad it gets, I wonder if I'll ever get it. Redemption, that's."

"Well, you saved Brian's life—numerous—times today," Michael said as he wiped his mouth and took a quick breath. "Anyone who would put their life on the line to save a stranger, especially a child, is a person who deserves redemption."

"Thanks, I appreciate that."

Brian looked up from his drawing, smiled but said nothing.

Michael shook his head. "Look, we all have a past, but it's the future you need to look toward—and know it starts with finding good friends, and you have two right here."

Brian looked up again. "Yeah, I hope you think of us as friends."

He'd be proud to be their friend. "Of course, I didn't think you'd want to be mine."

It sounded absurd, and even Brian knew it, rolling his eyes.

They laughed.

When looking at Michael and Brian, Mark felt something close to love. Admiration, maybe, or maybe it was just affection. Love.

"Michael, I just want you to know one thing."

"What's that?"

"You got a really good kid, and I know you're proud of him, and you should be, so take good care of him. One thing I've learned today is life's too short."

"Don't I see that now," Michael said. "Sad that it took something like this to see it, but it did."

Mark nodded with a full understanding.

"Do you have any kids?"

"No, and trust me, that's a good thing," Mark said. "Maybe in the future since my head's on a little straighter, but not now. I wasn't ready before, but I was also selfish. Just ask anyone. They'll tell you. Boy, will they ever. I cared for only myself and nobody else."

Eyeing his son. "I can't say how grateful I am you changed."

"Me too," Brian added.

Michael picked up his drink. "Toast." All three of them raised their glasses, and none contained alcohol. "To your new life. And may your journey be fruitful."

"Yeah, whatever that means, to new friends," Brian added.

Mark shook his head and smiled.

29

BAD NEWS

They finished eating and were about to leave when Agent Rothman entered the dining room and approached their table. Her face was tight, muscle-straining. Jaw twitching. She did not look pleased. Whatever she came to tell them— it wasn't gonna be good.

"Sorry to interrupt your dinner—"

"No problem," Michael interjected.

"—But we had a minor setback," she said, glancing at Brian, who stopped drawing to find out what was going on.

Mark knew by how she stressed the word *minor* that the setback was far from minor. Mark got Michael's attention and motioned with his eyes for them to leave.

Michael nodded. "You didn't interrupt. We were about to leave, then looked at his son," you ready, Brian?"

"Sure…if you are," Brian said with a smile, but his eyes

told Mark he was worried.

"So, how bad is it, anyway?" Mark asked as they got up to leave. "And don't worry about him; Brian can handle it."

"We didn't find him, but it was more than that. He's gone. His apartment was empty. Not one piece of furniture," Agent Rothman paused. "The other tenant said he was quiet and didn't bother anyone that he was barely home during the day, if at all."

"He wasn't really living there," Mark said." Believe me—I know the game. Usually, you keep a couch, a bed, and a TV."

"Why would you keep an apartment so bare?" Michael asked as they moved toward the exit.

Mark looked at Agent Rothman. "He was on parole or probation, wasn't he?"

Agent Rothman nodded. "Probation for about the last 18 months. It ended a week ago."

They exited through the plate glass door that opened to the parking lot. The chill of the night air sent shivers up their spines, which was exaggerated by fear of knowing he was still out there.

"Where's your car," Mark asked.

"It's around the corner, about a block or two away," she said.

Mark followed Brian's gaze upward. No moon. The sky was dark. Well, at least it stopped raining. It was probably the blackest night sky he had seen. The sidewalk along the front of the restaurant was packed. People still didn't feel safe riding public transportation, so they took to the streets. Mark couldn't blame them, only if they knew. Though some still rode the bus. A bus drove by with a handful of folks on it.

"I thought the buses stopped running?" Michael asked.

"We started them back up. He would've been looking for that."

"Suppose," Michael said.

"Still, it doesn't seem safe. Parker could've planted bombs on trains and buses set to go off remotely," Mark said. "And—"

A passing car backfired, making them all jump.

"Damn, that scared me," Mark said, "those buses make me nervous."

"Me too," Brian said in a voice barely a whisper. "Can we go now?"

"Yeah, sure, kiddo," his father said.

"Good idea," Mark said.

As they crossed the street, Mark looked at Brian and added, "I'm sorry. I shouldn't have said that."

"Nah, it's all right. I'm still a little nervous, but he thinks we're dead, right? So I'm okay. Besides, with you and my dad here. I feel safe."

Mark wished he could feel safe, but he couldn't as long as that dirtbag was still on the loose. He admired Brian. Some kids were so strong. Resilient. Mark just hoped it would be over soon.

They crossed in front of a bus stopped in bumper-to-bumper traffic, what another bus in front of them. Brian grabbed their hands for safety while walking between his father and Mark.

Michael and Mark exchanged a quick look but kept moving. On the other side, they continued up the street for a few blocks. The bus passed without incident. Mark would never admit it, but he held his breath the whole time until the buses passed. When Mark released his breath, he realized he wasn't alone. Brian and Michael were also holding their breath in.

They almost reached the corner when Michael's office building came into view. They would take this right to Agent Rothman's car a block away. Another bus crawled past—then stopped hard. They kept walking. A car in front of the bus had stalled. A beat-up Volvo. A standard. The gears grinding in protest as the driver tried to get the vehicle going. They passed the Volvo and reached the corner. Michael's office building, now in full view, looming overhead. The hackles at the back of his neck stood, and he looked back toward the bus—

In time to see it explode.

Mark snatched Brian up and pushed Michael around the corner as they stayed close to the building, using it as a shield. The blast still knocked them to the ground. Agent Rothman, slightly ahead of them, was untouched by the explosion. She drew her weapon and scanned the area, looking for Parker. Devastation lay in their wake. The bus was totally ripped apart. Mark, grief-stricken, felt for those who perished on the bus and around it. The scene was horrific. Cars flipped over, and people screamed. The brutality of the scene was by far the worst, but again, they had somehow escaped. He again was spared.

"What the fuck! You cowered!" Mark screamed, remembering Parker. "Show your face JJ. You fuckin cowered."

Agent Rothman pushed Mark toward her car. "Come on, we need to get them out of here!"

###

The following 20 minutes were a blur. Police and fire trucks passed them. Brian was hysterical and had taken most of the walk to Agent Rothman's car to calm him down. The kid was totally freaking out. Mark understood and was surprised it hadn't happened sooner because the entire day had been beyond terrifying. They got him into Agent Rothman's car and drove off.

The day's tragic events may not have been his fault, but he decided right there to finish it once and for all—before another innocent person died. There was just one question. One that he asked himself numerous times today. Mark didn't have the answer, but how the hell did he know where we were?"

"Do you have a leak in your office?" Michael asked Agent Rothman with a suspicious look.

"No—I don't think so; I hope not," she replied. Truly appalled.

Mark looked at Brian. They both changed their clothes. What was he missing? How would he do it if he needed to know someone's constant location? That's it. Got to be it. "Brian, give me your sneakers."

"What, why?" he said, taking them off and handing them to Mark anyway.

Agent Rothman turned down Michael's office building street.

Mark checked the first sneaker. Nothing. He checked the other and pulled out the sole. Dammit, nothing. It had to be there.

"What are you looking for?" Agent Rothman asked, looking in the rearview mirror at him.

"GPS," he said, "It has to be here."

Not willing to give up, he stuffed his hand into the size seven sneaker and slowly searched every inch of the insole.

Nothing. Then, on a whim, he checked the puffy tongue and smiled. He tore it open. "Found it."

"That fuckin bastard," Michael said.

"Agent Rothman?"

"Good job," she said. "What's up?"

"I need to ask you something."

"Sure anything," she said, eyeing him in the rearview mirror, "but first, how did you know?"

"I asked myself how I would do it. And I realized I would use a GPS tracking device. They're easy to buy, and some are tiny. He could have used geofencing, but he needed to ensure it would not get lost or destroyed in the explosion in case he missed."

"You have a plan, don't you?"

"Oh, I do," Mark said. The venom in those three little words scared the others.

Whether any of them would admit it—they knew Jonathan "JJ" Parker's days were numbered.

30

DEAD MY ARSE

Parker returned to O'Reilly's and sat at the bar, tossing back a beer. His cellphone sat next to his glass on the bar top. It lit up as the cellphone vibrated across toward him. He snatched it before it yeeted off the edge. He fumbled with it, all thumbs, before finding the call accept button.

"Hello?" He croaked into the phone. "Who's this?"

Parker's nerves quieted down when he realized it was just the rich kid calling to remind him to erase everything from the phone he held in his hand. The kid knew the rest of the plan and didn't want the phone traced back to him. Parker agreed to erase all the calls and data on the phone.

The GPS tracking program definitely had to go. A factory reset would set the phone back to its original state. Just a friendly reminder, that's all. The kid tried to talk him out of going through with his plan. Parker felt it touching, but he knew he didn't belong on this earth anymore, nor did he deserve to either.

"All right, kid, I'll make sure I do that before taking off," Parker said before pausing. "And I'll think about what you said as well, okay?"

The kid knew Parker was just blowing smoke up his ass, but it was nice that the kid didn't tell him so.

"All right, I gotta go," Parker said before ending the call.

The kid understood that he didn't want to go back to prison. The part of the plan where they didn't see eye to eye. They had taken extreme measures to alter his appearance because of it. Parker had seen his face several times during news reports. He felt good to know nobody would recognize him, especially those in prison who watched the television news religiously. He couldn't afford to get the dime dropped on him the first time he was seen on the screen.

Parker picked up the iPhone and deleted all the numbers, including the kids, but it was committed to memory, so it didn't need to be in the phone anyway. He had to go into the tracking program and close it out before deleting it.

He knew he was gonna reset the phone, but he still didn't trust anything, so he wanted to delete everything first. The kid told him it was redundant and unnecessary, but he didn't listen. Also, the data could be retrieved from a reset phone if the authorities decided to look, but he planned on dropping the phone somewhere where it would be snatched up within minutes.

He opened the program.

The blue dot moved.

Two hours after the explosion, the dot should not be moving. *Should it?* It didn't blink at the morgue or hospital. No. The location was near Brian's father's office building, and he watched as it moved away from the building.

He drained the rest of his beer.

Parker placed the empty mug on the counter and redialed the kid's number. The line rang twice before connecting. "They're still alive…" He filled the kid in on what he saw. The kid asked him for their current location and told him to stay put. He also told Parker he'd call him back.

Ten minutes and a couple of beers later, the kid called back. Parker kept his eyes on the blue dot the entire time. His anger rose until it boiled over the top. When the phone buzzed, he answered it. He told the kid the dot stopped moving and gave him the location. The kid was only a couple of blocks away. After several minutes of silence, the kid told him he had them in his sights…that they were, in fact, alive and well.

"All right, keep an eye on them, and I'll be right there."

The kid said he would and hung up.

Parker paid the bartender, picked up his cellphone, and left the bar.

After ten minute ride, the cab dropped him off in front of the address. It turned out to be a very exclusive restaurant. Parker looked around for the kid, but he didn't see him. His cellphone buzzed in his pocket.

"Where are you?"

The kid told him where he had parked. Parker looked in that direction and spotted him sitting in his car. He crossed the street. A moment later, he sat beside the kid in a Mercedes-Benz S Class.

"There in the restaurant?" Parker asked.

"Yeah, I watched them go inside," the kid said. "They haven't come out."

"That's good," Parker said, shaking his head. "Fucking cockroaches."

"They're certainly hard to kill, aren't they?"

"Yeah."

"Well, I don't know, maybe it's a sign—"

"No! They must die. It's just not gonna be the way I'd hope, that's all. Did you bring what I asked for?"

"Yeah, it's in the backseat."

Parker looked in the back. On the seat lay a large duffel bag. Initially, the kid had a bigger role but backed out, taking revenge on the people who murdered his family—only because someone else had beaten him to the punch. The kid didn't know who'd done it, but he was pleased someone had. Inside the bag was another vest loaded with plastic explosives like the one he placed on Brian. Also, there were six disks. He just hoped it would be enough. Nothing seemed to be enough to kill these cockroaches.

"Did you bring what else I asked for?"

He nodded toward the glove box. "Inside."

Parker opened the glove box to find a loaded Glock 9 mm.

"More ammo and extra mags are in the bag with the rest of the stuff."

Parker nodded. "Cool," he said as he removed the gun from the glove compartment and turned it over in his hands. He was in another place. His mind just couldn't wrap around the situation. No one should have been able to survive that many attempts on their lives. *Fucking nine lives.* He pulled

back the slide to check if there was one in the chamber—
there wasn't. He pulled it all the way back and let it go:
cha-chi-clack.

There was now.

He stuffed the gun in the front of his pants and pulled his
T-shirt down over it. Parker reached in the back, opened the
bag, and removed two disks. Without saying a word, he got out
of the car. Traffic on the street moved at an inchworm's pace.
As he walked away from the vehicle, he noticed the MBTA
buses were taking passengers. Though aboard the buses, he
only saw a few passengers. He walked to the bus stop a block
and a half away and waited. He removed his cellphone, called
the kid, and told him to get the van and come back. The kid
said he would. After he hung up the phone, Parker watched
the blue dot as it remained still. Almost an hour went by when
the dot moved toward the exit. He jumped on the next bus.

The bus slowly made its way down the congested street.
After setting the disk in two places, one at the back near the
engine and the other in front there the driver, he pressed
the stop button and got off the bus. He waited for the
bus to drive on. Across the street, at a 35° angle, he saw
Michael, Mark, the kid, and some lady. He wondered who
the woman was as he watched the quartet cross the street.
The bus slowly approached them.

He smiled. The street curved slightly, and Parker lost
sight of them. He removed his cellphone and placed the
call as he walked in their direction.

A car backfired up ahead, making Parker jump. Perfect,
he thought as he put his phone in his pocket. The bus slowly
approached the corner and then stopped. He could see

them again. The bus stopped, which bothered Parker, for the light at the intersection was green. He fell back, knowing what was to come. A brilliant light flashed out from where the bus stopped. The powerful explosion tore the bus into pieces and tossed cars near it aside.

Some of the cars had flipped onto their roofs. The street erupted in screams as panic took over the scene. People hit the pavement. The street was littered with people, both dead and alive. After checking the tracker and seeing the dot didn't move, he stuffed the phone into his pocket and fled the scene.

The blinking blue dot remained on the screen. If Parker had watched the screen a little longer, he would see the dot start to move—and undoubtedly, he would've cursed those "fucking cockroaches." Though he didn't trust that they were dead, he headed to a position where he could see himself. He had to see them dead with his own eyes.

31

COME TO ME

After dropping Brian and Michael off at his office building, Agent Rothman and Mark continued to drive to a part of town Mark once called home. A place he knew well. Where he also knew stood an empty building. The last occupant moved out six months before, which he knew because the warehouse was the only property he owned, having inherited from his uncle. And like his life, it was worthless. Two months after the last occupant left, the city condemned the building. To top it off, he couldn't sell it due to a problem with the soil. It meant he had to spend a ton of money before making anything on the property.

The building sat on almost two acres of land, and the warehouse took up most of the space. A small fenced-in yard was in the back. Inside was an office area, a two-door loading dock racing out the back. In between the front office and the loading dock was an enormous room. The current ceiling made the place look even larger than it was. Mark figured the place was ideal, considering there were no other buildings on either side of the property.

Mark led Agent Rothman through the office and onto the factory floor to the loading dock beyond. The factory once made candy. They passed through two huge double doors. One of which was open. The two garage doors leading to the loading dock were closed. He glanced around the room, empty except for several pallets that were left abandoned. Probably from the last tenant.

Mark hadn't been there in years. When he was a kid, perhaps ten or eleven, his father used to take him there when it still produced candy. He smiled at the fond memory. "Sorry, Pop," he whispered to the ghost of his father, "making you proud right now, aren't I? About time, huh?"

He headed for a shelf off to the left that ran across one wall. It kinda resembled a bookshelf. "This way."

"This way, where?" Agent Rothman said, perplexed. "There's nothing there."

"Through the door behind that shelf, which hasn't been used since my childhood when they hid my cousin Joe from the police. The room was created during prohibition back in the 1920s."

He approached the shelf, felt around the edges until he found what he was looking for, and pressed in the catch. They heard an audible click…he pulled on the shelf…and was rewarded with another click. He pushed it back as it swung inward.

Dust rose from every surface.

The small room beyond contained a staircase that led up to a secret room.

Agent Rothman coughed. "Why are you bringing me up there?"

Mark looked around. "Well, you can stay here, and I'll run upstairs with this," holding up the GPS unit. "And I'll put it in the center of the room and come right back down. It'll just take a minute."

"All right, go ahead and hurry up."

Mark ran up the stairs to the room above, and he was grateful that Agent Rothman decided to stay downstairs and would no longer have to feign ignorance. At the top of the stairs was a metal door. One that looked 80+ years old. More like seven. He turned the knob and pulled the door open. The room before him ran the length and width of the backroom downstairs. Complete darkness greeted him. The room had no windows. Mark stepped inside, flipped the light switch upward, and the room became awash with bright incandescent light.

The windowless room seemed to belong somewhere else—at least in a different era. Perhaps back in the 1920s, when it was a speakeasy.

Today, up until his uncle passed away, it was where Uncle Will kept his merchandise. The room was stacked with boxes and boxes. There were also hundreds of plastic containers of all shapes and sizes except round. Mark walked to the center of the room, where he placed the GPS device atop a stack of boxes. Then he turned his attention to the plastic containers that littered the place.

Most of the containers were about three or four feet long and a foot wide, but what he was looking for would be in a small container. He found what he was looking for stacked up against the back wall. He pulled out two containers and read the labels to make sure they were what he wanted—they were. He popped the latches and flipped back the lid.

"Nice," Mark said as he removed the FN Five-seveN and two magazines from the first case. He set the gun down and emptied the contents of the other container. He found the special 5.7 mm ammo that went with the weapons and removed several boxes. He hoped to find more magazines, but he did not but hoped it would be enough.

"Mark! What's taking so long?" Agent Rothman called from below.

"I'm coming. There's a restroom up here, and I needed to use it," he called back as he filled twenty rounds into each of the four magazines. He jacked a round into the chamber of each gun, added another round to each mag, and headed back downstairs after he stuffed the two guns that were no bigger than a Glock into his waistband.

"What took so long?" She asked.

"I told you I had to use the head, but I didn't think about if it still worked. It didn't. I'm just glad all I did was take a piss. Besides, I'm gonna have to tear this place down anyway. The city condemned it four months ago—there's a problem with the soil, so use is limited. Unless I can find the money to fix the problems, tearing it down is the cheaper thing to do and still expensive."

"If we don't keep an eye out for Parker," she said with a smile, "you won't have a building to fix."

"Are you kidding? I hope he does blow this place up," Mark smiled slightly. "I do have insurance."

"Oh, the truth comes out. You are a criminal."

"So says my record," he said as he returned to the factory floor. "We can watch the street from the office."

They crossed the expanse and entered the office.

"If you take that end, I'll take this end."

"Sounds good to me," Mark said.

They didn't have to wait long.

"I got some movement," Mark called.

"I see him," Agent Rothman said. "It's him, isn't it?"

"Looks like him to me," he said. "Now what?"

"We watch him—I lost sight of him."

"I got him. He's following the signal. Now he's going out-back. He keeps looking at the building. Looking for a way in, I suppose."

Agent Rothman came up behind him. "Or a place to set charges."

"Or that," Mark said, hoping the place wouldn't blow up. All the ammo upstairs would cause a lot of problems. It wouldn't be good.

Mark left the room, caught up with Agent Rothman, and whispered, "You got me talking to myself back there."

"Sorry," she whispered back.

A gust of cold air rushed into the big room.

"I think he found a way in," she said.

Agent Rothman held up her finger to her lips. He got the message. Be silent. She motioned for him to watch out the window for Parker as she drew her Glock and headed into the back room.

She entered the backroom when Mark caught sight of Parker coming their way. Parker stopped right before the window and placed something on the building. This wasn't good. Mark ran to the front of the building, back through the office, and out the front door. Once outside on the side-walk, Mark drew both automatics and headed for the side of the building.

Mark had already decided how this was going to end. It might not have been Mark's fault, but it was about Jonathan JJ Parker and his actions.

Now and back in prison.

Mark remembered the incident, long since forgotten, but if he'd finished it back then, he wouldn't be in the position he now found himself. There wouldn't have been so much destruction—and innocent lives lost.

It all began when Mark had first gone upstate. Back then, everyone went to MCI-Concord for intake. Most of the people who went there were young and came from county facilities before going to their permanent institution.

While in the county, they were fed misinformation, including Mark, about how the stay in prison would be. The rules, if you will. Every day in the county, you heard: "You can't do that upstate." or "Say something like that upstate, you'll get stuck." Basically, people who had never done time in a state prison told you how it would be. Even the people who had gone seemed to get it all wrong. When Mark arrived, it wasn't anything like he expected. At least not how people in the county believed, and it didn't surprise him.

Mark did Mark; he wasn't surprised to see people using their manners, mainly from those who had done time in prison or otherwise. But those who came from the county waiting classification just didn't have a clue. Mark suspected they watched too many prison movies as they walked around with their chests puffed out, faces twisted up, looking mean. *Scared to death.*

Jonathan Parker, known as JJ to those in the yard, was no exception. He moved into this kid's cell named Robert Redman. Bobby was a good kid who just made a stupid decision, crashing his car while drag racing, injuring some young kid. Melanie's law was new then, so they made an example out of Bobby.

The kid was a natural at doing time. Nobody had anything bad to say about him. Though some may argue Mark had something to do with that.

The kid was only 19, had about two years left on a five-year bid, and had most of his time done. The kid had no problem, at least that is, until Jonathan Parker moved into his cell. Parker carried a massive chip on his shoulder and immediately tried to get Bobby to shoulder some of the weight.

Listening to idiots and believing what they told him to be fact, JJ tried to press his newfound views on others, such as whites should only hang with their own kind. Never should a black and a white live in the same cell, and if the screws put one in your cell, you better stick him.

It was absurd that someone would propagate segregation and hate in the Massachusetts prison system in the 21st century. In Massachusetts, you bunked with whomever, you had no choice, so it made no sense. For the most part, this view wasn't the case except for a small ignorant crowd of white dudes.

Mark had a straightforward rule: show me respect, and he'd do the same. Presence was not enough. Nobody needed unnecessary headaches. Bad enough, classism ran rapid throughout the place. Many of the convicts didn't have people on the outside, so they didn't have any money. Bobby was one such person.

The prisoners had to find something to occupy their time during lock-ins—the kid used the time to draw greeting cards for canteen. Of course, JJ had a medical bottom bunk pass that he didn't need, and he didn't like Bobby drawing at the desk all day. He expected the kid to stay up on his bunk. Hell, he didn't like anything the kid did, telling him his drawings weren't any good when they were better than good. He was just a hater. He would tell him to pull up his pants and that if he wanted to dress like a n#@!r, he could move in with one. The ER couldn't get any more pronounced—a shotgun blast off the second syllable.

Despicable.

The incident happened not long after JJ moved into the kid's cell. JJ was a pretty big guy but on the heavy side. He had gone to the gym, and when he returned, he found this kid Tyson inside his cell talking to Bobby—and the big dude flipped.

"What the fuck, kid," he shouted. "You know I don't like anybody inside the cell, man. That's total disrespect—"

"Hold the fuck up," Tyson said. "What you yelling at this man for? It's as much his cell if not more, seeing Bobby was here first."

"I don't believe I was talking to *you*," JJ said. "This is between my cellie and me, got it?" He poked his finger in Tyson's chest.

Tyson had balls and would stand up for himself no matter what, but even he knew when he was outmatched. "Look," Tyson said, trying to fix the situation. "My fault, I needed a card for my mom, and I apologize."

JJ just stood there staring at Bobby with his face all twisted up. Bobby knew JJ was gonna blow up on him later.

Bobby stood, picking up his drawing supplies. "Come on, Tyson, I'm sure my cellie wants to change to go take a shower."

They went to the day room, but there were only about five minutes left of rec time. Tyson's friend, Dominic, didn't have a cellmate because he had gotten lugged the night before.

Tyson and his friends had Bobby's back. Dominic said he could move into his cell, seeing there was a bed open. Bobby figured any place was better than living with JJ, but he wanted to talk to Mark first, but Dom had already asked the CO.

"Redman, if you gonna move," he called across the rec room. "You gotta do it now or not at all."

"Come on," Tyson said. "We'll help you."

Tyson's three friends agreed.

JJ was still in the shower when Bobby started to move out. Bobby hoped JJ would be in the cell, so he could tell him he was moving out, but the guy was just a pain in the ass. So it really didn't matter.

"Go, just grab your stuff," Dominic said, handing Bobby a trash bag. "Put your shit in the bag, and you can sort it out later."

"Yeah, little dude, let's just get you out of that cell," one of the big dudes said.

Within five minutes, most of Bobby's stuff was down the tier inside Dominic's cell. JJ approached the cell, seeing four brothers, one of which was inside his cell. He fumed, thinking the kid was again disrespecting him.

"What the fuck, kid! I—"

He cut himself off, realizing what was going on.

"What're you doing?" JJ asked.

"Moving out," Bobby said matter-of-factly.

"For what, kid," he said, his face a mask of anger. "I think you're blowing this all out of proportion."

"Am I," the kid said, feeling safe in the presence of the three big guys. "Shit, if I wanted to live with my father, I wouldn't have ran away when I was twelve. If truth be told, he wasn't all that bad. At least he didn't put everything I did down."

"Whoa, kid," JJ said, glaring at Bobby. "Don…"

"Bobby, I know you're mad, and you feel disrespected," Dominic said, "but don't do the same to him."

JJ eyed the three black dudes. He didn't need their kind's help. Hell, he shouldn't have been locked up in the first place, especially for life. Not for what he did. He killed the person he *knew* killed his son. That motherfucker got off, and in Jonathan's opinion, because the man was black.

He turned his attention back to Bobby, who now had the last of his belongings in his hands. *Good riddance.* Still, he was pissed more because of the black dudes than anything. The three dudes disgusted him and would, no matter their color. He heard Dominic killed a kid. His own fucking child. JJ couldn't understand someone doing that. Though heinous, the others were worse, according to what he heard.

The biggest guy, Reggie, tried to rape a young boy. He hated pedos. And he couldn't understand why nobody did anything to get him off the block, and Darrell, Tyson's cousin, used to prostitute little girls. They were all scumbags, and he didn't care if the rumors were true or not—he believed them, and that was all that mattered.

Of course, nothing his boys told him held any truth—just rumors spread by racist pieces of shit, trying to get people to hate them for nothing.

The next afternoon in the yard, Bobby walked with Mark, telling him about what happened and why he moved out. JJ had been running Bobby's name in the dirt ever since. It wouldn't have been a big deal if they hadn't moved a brother into JJ's cell. The man was massive—solid muscle and at least four inches taller than JJ's 6' 2" frame. On top of it, he was respected. The big man had a reputation for doing most of his time the hole. When someone asked about it, he simply said, "I like to fight."

At the chow hall, JJ complained about his new cellmate. One of his boys, a kid named Danny, called him out. "You said if a brother moved in, you'd take care of him—so take care of him. You got a problem; take care of it."

JJ nodded. "Yeah, you're right. A man's gotta do what a man's gotta do."

Word made it back to Bobby—he decided to stay close to Mark. Indeed, he was the only person he could trust.

"So, you think he's gonna do it?"

"Stick his cellie; I doubt it," Mark said. "Man, never said shit to you when I was around. Personally, I think he's a coward, so yeah, he's probably gonna do something grimy, but only because he's scared."

"All right," Bobby said. "I see some friends, so I'm going to take off."

Mark raised his arms and sniffed under each armpit. "What, do I smell or something?"

"Definitely the or-something."

"Oh, I see," Mark said, pushing the kid. "Because I'm walking too fast, isn't it?"

"Dude, you're practically running, and I don't do that either, see you around."

Mark wouldn't see Bobby again unless he went to the cemetery where he was buried. Mark had arranged with Jimmy's mother to use his own plot. Mark did a couple more laps. One was on the opposite end of the plus-size football field—he saw a commotion going on near the handball courts, and he was near the basketball and volleyball court on the other end.

The guards rushed the field.

Everyone was ordered to leave the yard—the announcement coming over the loudspeakers. Mark instantly looked for Bobby, who couldn't be found in the crowd. When he got back to the block, he searched the unit, hoping to find the kid already back there. He ran into Dominic, who had the look of someone suffering loss. Mark didn't need to be told.

"Who?"

Dominic nodded.

Mark looked behind him and saw JJ standing in the doorway to his cell. Anger rose as he approached JJ.

What happened next was a blur. Mark pushed a stunned JJ backward into his cell. Seeing Mark's anger, his cellmate stepped by Mark to leave the tiny cell. As he left, he looked back at JJ and smiled. "Have a good time, fellas."

JJ took this moment to launch at Mark, grabbing him around the waist. Before JJ could get a firm hold on to him,

Mark brought an elbow down hard on the base of JJ's neck with all his weight and strength. JJ released his grip and crashed hard to the concrete floor. He winced in pain. He tried to scramble to his feet, but it was too late. Mark shot his leg straight up in the air and brought the crescent kick down with enough force to break five two-inch-thick patio bricks. The big man didn't have a chance—lights out. Thinking the dumbass got the message, Mark went back to his cell.

For three days, there was no word on Bobby's condition. During that time, JJ avoided Mark like the plague—if Mark entered a room, JJ exited. The word came: Bobby had died. That's when everything changed. JJ knew he had to get Mark before Mark got him. Parker got his chance a few days later outside the chow hall. The line to enter to get your food went outside. Right outside the door to the building was a blind spot, one not always watched by the guards and wasn't on this day.

JJ came from behind a dumpster outside the door, wielding a shank aiming for Mark's kidneys. Mark somehow saw the movement behind him and spun around. The speed at which someone his size shouldn't be able to achieve. Thrusting his left hand straight out, striking JJ dead in the throat, then with his right, he connected a powerful palm heel strike to JJ's nose. Blood exploded from his nostrils as the cartilage crunched grotesquely.

He dropped the shank, and it clanged away from them.

JJ flailed his arms, trying to strike at Mark, who grabbed JJ's right arm and twisted it roughly while simultaneously striking the elbow with his palm and pushing until…it snapped like a twig. JJ howled in agony. Mark took out his legs and stood over him. He leaned over JJ and struck him in the face. Immediately, he screamed for Mark to stop. Several guards appeared and ordered Mark to stop before two of them tackled him to the ground.

Mark thought about taking JJ's life for Bobby's from the first strike. *Life for a life.* But the good that dwells in all of us prevailed, and Mark let the monster live. Besides, at the time, JJ was doing life without parole. He believed JJ would never see the street again. About a year later, Mark heard the jackass had overturned his case, and he was now convicted of manslaughter, not murder. As he now knew, he got out 18 months ago with a plan to cause extreme harm.

Mark's pace quickened, and his eyes narrowed at the memory. Two more long strides, and he'd reached the corner and end it—for good. He turned the corner, raising the lethal weapons, and caught the dumbass coming toward him. JJ's eyes widened as he stopped dead.

"This time, you get what you deserve," Mark said, double tapping both triggers. JJ tried to scramble out of the way, but the fence on one side and the concrete wall on the other prevented any such plan. The first two shots got him in the torso while the other two missed. Mark squeezed off more rounds. He still tried to scramble back the way he came. Two more shots went through the man's coat. He fell and scrambled back to his feet and fell again. Before Mark knew it, both guns jacked open. JJ lay sprawled on the ground—motionless. Mark wasn't trusting the son of a bitch. He dumped the two mags and loaded fresh ones—and jacked a round into each chamber.

"Mark!" Agent Rothman called from within the building.

He bent down to check JJ's pulse. He was still alive. Agent Rothman's voice saved Parker from imminent death. He left Parker and went down the alley to the back. Agent Rothman met him as he turned the corner and pointed a gun at him.

"Jesus," she said, lowering her weapon. "I almost shot you." Then she noticed the two weapons. "Not even going to ask. Did you get him?"

"Look for yourself," he said, pointing back to the alley. "He's righ—"

She looked around the corner. He was gone.

"Fuck, he couldn't have gotten far. I hit him at least ten times."

"Ten times—"

"He has to be wearing a vest," he said, "but this ammo is armor-piercing. It should've gone through. Enough to stop him, anyway."

"He couldn't've gotten far. Let's go."

They ran to the front of the building. Agent Rothman noticed a trail of blood leading to the right. "I got blood," she said and motioned in the direction. A block away, they saw a man stumbling across the street. "We got him; come on."

JJ crossed the street and got into a van.

They ran toward the plain white van and made it 20 feet before a blinding white light washed over them, causing them to close their eyes. The van exploded and stopped them dead in their tracks.

32

THE MORNING AFTER

After Jonathan JJ Parker blew himself to nonexistence, there were many, many questions to be answered. Agent Rothman's superiors arrived on the scene—wanting answers, especially how an ex-con, never mind a suspect in the matter, came to be the last person to see Parker alive. They also wanted to know where Mark got the guns. To Mark's surprise, Agent Rothman said she didn't know and that the weapon probably belonged to his deceased uncle, who left the property to him.

Agent Rothman could have hung him out to dry, but she hadn't. She seemed to see him in a different light as if they belonged to the same race as something. Mark knew, however, that she only had his back because, not for nothing, they were on the same side this time.

Hours of questioning lasted all night from several different agents—and even the same ones at other times. It all felt like hell. At first, they acted like they were gonna pin everything on him: setting up the attack, using Parker as a scapegoat, and executing everything from his prison cell. Though this story didn't fly, it rattled Mark. He knew for once he was on the right side. And to Mark, one who would never snitch, killing Parker was the only option—if there were any. By 5:30 AM, they realized his story wasn't gonna change, so they let him go.

Once he left the small one-way mirrored interrogation room, he realized why he had been let go. Standing in the waiting room was Agent Rothman. She looked disheveled. Her shirt was untucked, her hair out of the tight bun she kept it in. Her whole appearance made her look exhausted. The higher-ups put her through the same wringer.

She made a gesture toward the next room. "Brian and his father are in there."

Mark checked his watch for the time. 5:03 AM.

"Shit, we've been here almost nine hours," Mark said and shook his head. "How long have they been in there?"

"For at least four hours."

"What the fuck's going on," Mark said through clenched teeth. "Fucking idiots! Do they understand the trauma Brian's endured?"

"And you," Agent Rothman said.

"Stuff like that doesn't bother me much anymore," Mark said, trying to force a smile. "Call it a byproduct of the environment I've lived in for the last several years."

"Shit has to affect you—you're still human, aren't you?"

The door to the next room opened, giving Mark a reprieve from answering Angela's question. Brian, Michael, and a woman exited the room. Mark brightened when he saw that Brian looked good—and smiling. The kid didn't look tired at all. But his father, on the other hand, looked as he supposed he and Angela both looked: beaten-up and exhausted. Brian saw Mark and broke free from his father.

He ran to Mark and hugged him. Mark smiled. "What's going on, little man. Are you guys done too?"

"Yeah," Brian said, then looked back to the woman who approached them.

"You must be Mark," she said, extending a hand. "I'm Margaret Sawyer. I was asked to come to evaluate Brian's mental state. They wanted to know if what he said could be relied upon."

"There's no way—"

She held up her hand. "Stop. We know…I believe Brian and I told them that though there are signs of trauma, it was lessened because of Brian's faith, which was enhanced, I might add, because of you."

"Oh…well…thank you," Mark said. "I thought those jerks had been questioning him this whole time."

"They were, sort of, but under my watchful eye," she winked. "It is very nice to have met you. Keep going. You're on the right road."

"What road is that, may I ask?" he said, sounding more contrite than defensive.

She smiled. "The one to redemption."

Dr. Sawyer turned to say goodbye to Michael and Brian, still attached to Mark, and left.

"She seemed nice," Mark said. He looked down and patted Brian on the back. "Come on; you gotta let me go so we can get out of here." Brian released him in a nanosecond, and the three of them headed for the door. Mark turned back, looking over his shoulder at Agent Rothman. "You coming or what?"

"Yeah, why not."

"So, who's up for breakfast?" Mark asked.

Of course, Brian was, and that was all that mattered.

An hour later, they were back at Michael's office. Agent Rothman had just left. She had a ton of paperwork to finish but first wanted to go home to freshen up before going back to work. Mark and Michael were talking while Brian sat in the left corner of the office next to one of the floor-to-ceiling windows drawing. Brian had taken it into the restaurant when they ate breakfast and had been quietly drawing since interjecting his comments in adult conversation when he deemed necessary.

When Mark looked at the quiet, well-behaved boy, he saw a strong person and hoped the day's events didn't weigh too heavily upon him, so Brian could grow up to be a great adult. The boy inspired those around him, especially Mark, with his ability to see the good in people—and hold to it. He watched Brian draw, which he saw as the kid's means of escape.

"Hey, Lil man, what are you drawing over there?"

Brian looked up at Mark, rolled his eyes, and said, "Duh, a picture." Then he smiled before a fit of giggles consumed him.

The boy was going to be all right, Mark thought.

"Funny, so what are you drawing?

"I'm drawing something for you; no, you can't see it. I'm almost finished. I'll show you in a minute.

"Sounds good."

Michael and Mark talked for a few moments until Brian brought over his masterpiece. Mark was taken aback by the quality of the work. Many guys locked up could draw, but he never saw anything as good as Brian's drawings.

"Wow, this is good. Hell, it's better than good," Mark declared, showing it to Michael.

He wasn't sure what he had expected to see, but it wasn't the picture before him. Brian perfectly captured Mark's image. What really took him aback was that Brian drew Mark as he saw him—as a hero. A superhero minus the Cape and the skintight clothing. He flipped through the pages of the book. There were twenty lifelike drawings. All of them were of Mark doing something heroic. The last one was of him at the restaurant while they ate breakfast, but it also had everyone else in it as well, including Agent Rothman. Mark couldn't draw stick figures if he tried, but he knew a talented artist when he saw one.

"So this is how you see me?" Mark asked, curious.

"Of course," Brian replied with a puzzled facial expression that screamed as if there was any other way one should see Mark—other than the hero he was.

"He's been drawing in that book since we got back to the office."

"Really?"

Brian smiled. "Do you like them?"

"Sure do. Which one can I have?" That puzzled look again. "All of them, stupid."

Mark set the book on the desk, scooped Brian up, and flipped him upside down. "I'm stoopid, huh? Well, how stoopid are you feeling right now for saying something like that?"

"Stop. Please. Stop," Brian half screeched and laughed.

"If that's what you want," Mark said as he set Brian down.

Brian dropped into Mark's chair. "Hey, you want to play some video games?"

"That's a good idea," Michael said. "There's no sense in going home now, at least for me, so I'm going to take a shower and change these clothes. After, we have something we want to talk to you about." Mark started to speak. "No, not now; it can wait until after."

Mark and Brian played some alien war game they could play as a team. They both had fun, and Mark wondered if this was how it felt to have a son...and if he would ever have one. Not that long ago, he would have thought not, but as he looked at Brian, he felt he would someday. He also knew that Brian and Michael would be a part of his son's life and his for a long time to come. They played video games for almost an hour, so Michael came out of the bathroom, looking like the high-powered attorney he was.

"All right, fellas, let's have that conversation. Brian, do you want to ask him, or do you want to?"

"You, I guess," he said, pausing the video game before going to his father's side.

Michael tousled his son's hair. "We talked this over at great length earlier, and we hope you will accept our offer. After what happened today, I realized my job can put my family and me," nodding down at Brian, "in danger, and Brian had already asked if I could get him a driver. At least for the next few weeks, and I told him I would look into the possibility of hiring security personnel to be at home when he's there alone. But he flat out refuses to let me do that," Brian smiled, "but he said there is one person who could do both, and he wouldn't fight me on it—if that person were you."

"You want me to be his driver and bodyguard?"

"No," Brian said. "I want you to be part of our family, but being my driver and bodyguard just comes with it."

Mark smiled. "I don't know. It still sounds like you want me to drive some spoiled rich kid around."

Michael laughed long and hard. "Well, the pay is good, say 80 grand a year plus full health benefits and a retirement package."

Mark laughed. "Hell, I'd do it for free."

"Oh, really?"

"But not as long as you're paying. It probably should be $100K."

They all laughed.

# # #

Mark still had to obtain a license due to the length of time he spent in prison. Brian and Mark put on their coats to leave. Michael tried to hand him some money, but he told Michael he had enough for now. He could pay for the taxi ride to their house. The job came with a room as well. He couldn't have hoped for more.

They raced to the elevator after they said bye to Michael. Brian acted like an average goofy twelve-year-old, making

Michael and Mark happy. He wasn't going to school that day because Michael decided to keep him out for the next few days. This way, he could show Mark where they live and where he'd be living as well. The elevator's doors dinged open.

"I'm so happy you accepted my dad's offer," Brian said. "Because I was afraid, I would never see you again if you didn't."

"Is that why you put him up to this?"

"Who, me?" Then he burst into a fit of contagious laughter.

Mark couldn't help but join in. "Come on, Lil man, let's go home."

"That sounds good."

They exited the building. Mark tried to wave down the first taxi he saw, but it drove right by. A taxi pulled away from the curb just up the block, its on-duty lights flashing on. Mark waved the car over.

"Here we go," he said as the taxi pulled over. Mark opened the door, and Brian jumped in. Mark followed behind.

"Where you...going?" The Indian accented voice asked.

Mark looked toward the driver and only saw the cabbie's eyes in the rearview mirror. Brown but almost black. Not the light-colored eyes of a ghost. Parker's death had been confirmed, but Mark was still suspicious. He also wondered if Parker had an accomplice—and if Parker did, where was this person now? Mark could tell Brian wanted to tell the driver.

"Go ahead, tell him."

Brian told the driver the address as he secured his seatbelt, and the doors locked as they pulled away from the curb. Indian music played softly on the radio. Soon they would be home.

33

NO MORE RICH KID

The white van bumped along the deserted street. Parker sat in the passenger seat, riding shotgun, and glanced at the tiny screen of the iPhone.

They were getting close.

"What's the address?" The rich kid asked.

"1753," he replied. "Will be on the right."

The van continued down the street.

"Is that it?" The kid said, pointing at a two-story warehouse. "I think that's it."

The faded numbers above the entrance agreed.

Parker urged the kid to drive past and turn around. They went by the building one more time and parked several buildings away on the opposite side of the street. He grabbed a couple of disks and stuffed them in his pockets.

"All right, stay here," Parker said. "If you see something,

anything, honk that fucking horn."

"Yeah, sure, Parker, if I see something."

"Good," Parker said as he got out of the van.

Parker crossed over to the other side. The warehouse mostly took up the street, and there was next to no traffic. Although cars were parked on the street, he'd only seen one in operation since turning onto the road. He approached the building with caution. He held the iPhone in his left hand and the handgun in the other. According to the position of the glowing blue dot, the boy was in the back of the building. His intuition told him something wasn't right, but he pushed it back because nothing had gone right all day. He didn't expect it to change now. He would check out the building and see if he could find a way inside that wouldn't alert anyone inside to his arrival.

As he approached the building, he noticed an alley on the left side, so he turned right into the alley, walking slowly along the width of the building. There was a fence on one side and the building on the other. The space between the two was narrow. It was barely enough space for him to walk. He crept to the back of the building, where he found a small dock and two garage doors. He walked around the building back to the front. On the other side, he found the driveway and not much of anything else. There were several windows, but most were too high off the ground for him to reach. However, there was a ground-level window near the end of the alley. The front also had a window, but if this were a setup, as he suspected, that would be the way he'd be expected to come and precisely why he needed to find another way in.

He made one more circuit around the building. However, this time around, he considered the building's structure and placed the disks in the right place to cause the most structural damage but kept it contained to the front of the building. That way, he could sneak into the back and take care of the brat. This time he'd put…two bullets into the kid's head…to ensure the deed was finally done. Once and for all. He came back through the alley.

As he made his way to the low window, his way in, he kicked up a good-sized rock…sending it hurling toward the window. Before Parker could react, the stone smashed through the windowpane, causing a cacophony of shattered glass. The sound interrupted the quiet neighborhood. Parker stopped in his tracks. He listened for a moment. Nothing. He hoped to hear movement inside. The building, but he didn't hear a thing. He checked the GPS. The dot remained motionless. The same spot. Good.

Since it already made enough noise to raise the dead, he removed the rest of the broken window when his foot. He crouched down and peered inside. The basement was dark, but the window provided enough light for him to see the room. It was small. He heard a door slam, ascending footfall…coming his way. Parker stood in time to see the assailant turn the corner with two guns raised in his direction—

Mark!

—Two flashes of light followed by a deafening sound. Then again. Parker, who had no place to run because the chain-link fence was too high, chose to zigzag toward the back of the building. Bullets burned past his head. Two tore through his coat, and several more dotted his back, sending him to the ground. He landed heavily on his side, and his head smashed against the asphalt. Unconsciousness quickly fell upon him.

A few minutes later, he came to with a start. He opened his eyes, expecting to see Mark on him, but what he found was no one. Parker looked around. He was alone. However, he could hear voices coming from the back of the building. He dragged himself to his feet. His back and abs hurt like hell. As he made his way out of the alley, he took inventory of the damage. It was hard to breathe, so he was sure he'd broken a rib or two. A bullet had struck him in the thigh, making his escape slow going. But he made it to the van. He slid the sliding door open, climbed, stumbled into the van, and closed the door.

"Jesus Christ, the kid said. I didn't have time to honk—"

"Don't worry about it."

"— Oh, shit! Here they come," the kid shouted. "There's two of them!"

Parker, who had removed his jacket, shirt, and vest, was bare-chested. "He tossed the bulletproof vest onto the floor. He managed to pull on a T-shirt when an annoying beeping sound pierced his eardrums.

"What's that sound?" He said, frustrated. "That beeping?"

"What!"

"Never mind, why aren't you driving," he shouted at the kid. "Let's go. Go, go, go!"

The kid mumbled something as he put the van into drive.

Parker found the source of the offending noise. His iPhone.

It pocket-dialed a number. When Parker saw the nine digits, he screamed. "Get out! Okay, stop the van and get out."

He unlocked the back door and pushed the double doors open.

"What do you mean stop?" The kid said in protest.

Parker's overly focused brain urged him to flee. And he did just in time. He leapt out the back of the van as the kid tried to pull over and park but never made it. Somehow, Parker managed to crawl under a car parked behind them before the van became engulfed in bright white light.

Pieces of metal rained down upon the street.

34

THE LAST SHOT

Burning hot debris lay scattered around him. The blast had sent the car he hid under crashing into the one behind it. He crawled until he made it clear. Along the way, he burned his leg on something that sizzled the skin. He also managed to burn his forearm when he pulled himself free from under the parked car.

He pulled himself to his feet and surveyed the damage. Smoke and fire filled the air. Debris from the band laid about. The smoke became too thick to see through.

Sirens pierced the air, bringing Parker out of shock and back to reality.

Parker turned from the devastation and ran to safety. His mind raced with statistics. He kept reaching up to his throbbing head to quell the shards of stabbing pain. What were the odds of your own phone pocket-dialing the number that could've killed you? The question stuck in his head as he ran several blocks until he saw a Boston Cab and flagged it down. He neither knew nor cared where he was headed as long as it was away from there. Nothing had gone right, but he planned. It just didn't make any sense to him. He knew he was right, that this needed to be done. Society needed to see the truth. They did. But why was everything going so wrong? So drastically wrong. He shook it off. It wasn't him…no…it was not him, but he knew who had fucked up everything for him…and always had. Mark. FUCKING MARK. Anger swelled in his chest as it spread and seeped through every pore. He pulled out the cell and checked the GPS, but the dot didn't move. Time to change the game on them. Switch things up a little bit so that he can regain the high ground and finish what he started.

With no other place to go, Parker went to the rich kid's luxurious digs. He figured it would take a while for the police to identify the remains. He hardly doubted there was anything left after that explosion. Besides, the kid wasn't using his actual ID. He had the whole works done: Driver's license, credit cards, and working passport. In fact, Parker never knew the kid's real name. When he wrote to him in prison, he used a different name. One that couldn't later be traced back to him. Parker knew he could hide at the Brookline mansion for as long as needed.

He'd only been to the mansion three times. The last time had been a week ago. Not only was it the most recent visit, but it was also the longest. The driveway was long, but the house came into view. He was awestruck as he had been the other time. The house was grand. He headed for the main entrance. Parker knew the kid lived there alone and bought the house and its contents the year before. The kid had mentioned that he'd never met a single neighbor. "The filthy rich like their privacy," he told Parker not that long ago.

To his amazement, the door was unlocked. After entering, he looked for an alarm but found none. He headed to the kitchen, where he found a control panel for the alarm on the wall to the left of the doorway, the light on it a steady green. It had never been set. With a sense of relief, he grabbed a beer out of the fridge before heading upstairs to get ready.

Everything he needed was upstairs.

As he climbed the stairs, he realized he only had two disks on him. He checked his pockets. Instead of two, he found none. Then he realized what had happened. He had taken off the jacket and shirt to remove the bulletproof vest. Before the explosion, he was able to put on a T-shirt but not his jacket. Somehow, in the chaos, he'd forgotten. He walked into the kid's bedroom and headed straight for the bathroom and a shower.

Ten minutes later, he got out of the shower, dried off, and slid on boxes before entering the walk-in closet from the bathroom. He selected another T-shirt and a pair of black jeans along with black socks and a pair of appropriate shoes. He brought the new attire to the bedroom. He set the clothes down on the bed and sat on a bench at the foot of the bed. He looked around the room. *This would be the life.*

Parker got dressed and sat heavily on the bed as something hefty slid from under the pillow and smacked the base of his head. He winced in pain.

"What the fuck," he yelled to the empty room as he scooped up the object.

He felt the round shape in his palm and knew what it was. A smile edged at the corners of his mouth. Uncontrollably, he laughed. The sound echoed throughout the empty house. He held the disk and began tossing it back and forth in his hands. Finally, something had gone his way. It was only one, but it would have to do.

Besides, he had managed to hold on to the Glock, but there were more guns and ammo in the house. The kid had a gun permit. He was an avid collector. Parker also knew the kid bought some weapons off the street because he had set it up. Like the one he gave Parker. Finding the guns and extra ammo would have to wait. First, he needed to change his appearance.

Parker checked himself in the mirror before he left the room. He walked down a wide hallway to a suite of rooms. The kid's studio where he made Parker another man. The latex-based paint that covered Parker's entire body would not wash off. It would wear away over several weeks. The only part of him that wasn't painted was the pads of his hands, the soles of his feet, and his jewels, of course.

He figured nobody would look that closely, and if he got arrested, he knew the cops wouldn't, either. Some not at all. Hell, would you want to? He knew he didn't. The kid would bail him out before the fingerprints came back because he didn't have any.

A bank account was set up in a false name with over 5 million dollars, the account Parker used to draw funds.

If Parker wanted to disappear to a place where nobody would ever find him, he could with ease. But that wasn't part of the plan. Now…more than ever…he had to see it to the end—to finish what he started so the rich kid's death wouldn't be in vain. Though many people now suffer the loss of loved ones, it wasn't enough. Not as far as he was concerned. It wouldn't be enough until Michael also suffered because his son was gone. Buried. *Dead*.

He sat at the makeup desk. The kid showed him how to do touchups. Parker had gotten pretty good at it. He'd redone his entire face once, but the kid was right there giving directions. This would be his first solo flight. He was on his own. Parker picked up the airbrush and attached the cup, and began. He started with his face, which didn't take much but a thin coat of the latex mixture—the kid's own recipe.

Twenty minutes later, his face was no longer that of an African-American. He was slightly lighter, with the reddish hue making him look Indian. The only thing missing was the red dot. Parker wasn't sure if men wore it. The look, however, did inspire an idea. A brilliant, if not a stereotypical one. If for no other purpose, it would allow him to survey his prey undetected. Now, where were they hiding? Home? Office? Parker was sure it would be one of them. It was late, so they were probably home feeling safe.

He chuckled at the thought.

When he finished his makeup, he decided to check out the news. There was a flat-panel TV on the wall, and he turned it on. Parker resumed with finishing touches to his face and neck. When an anchor appeared on the screen, talking about the day's tragic events, he ignored it mostly.

Until that is, the reporter proclaimed the bomber had taken his own life in a terrific explosion. He swiveled around in the chair to face the TV and focus on the report.

"There are very few details at the moment," the reporter said. "but from what our sources gathered, the man took his own life after being caught in a setup devised by the agent-in-charge. The bomber was shot though the circumstances are unclear. The man made it to his vehicle parked nearby; once inside, the man knew it was over. The authorities knew who he was, so it was only a matter of time before they caught him. There was nowhere to run. As we can see from the Skynews cam, debris from the bomber's vehicle is scattered about the street. The end to a day Bostonians will never forget…for a long time. This is a sad day for us all," this is Jean Broward for Faux 25. Back to you, Stacy."

The screen flashed back to the news desk.

Parker switched the TV off and spun around to check himself in the mirror. Satisfied, he moved on to his hands. Five minutes later, the look was complete. He stood. It was now time to find ammo for the Glock.

The house was big, but the kid had told him that he mostly stayed on the second floor because everything he needed was there—all his toys. He only needed to go downstairs to get something from the kitchen. Parker checked the suite of rooms and came up empty. He returned to the master bedroom.

The main compartment of the suite, the sleeping quarters, had three walls. Nothing could be hidden behind them. But to get to the sleeping quarters, he had to pass through a small anteroom. He was sure the room held no secrets, but it abutted the walk-in closet, which he thought might. He rummaged through the masculine closet the size of a large bedroom.

The walk-in was a squat rectangle—almost a square in appearance. Elaborate built-in units comprising drawers and shelves occupied two walls. He knew the wall to the left was external. While the one ahead, he had no clue. The closet had two entrances. The one in which he had just come in and from the master bath. The room beyond the right wall. The only wall that could hold a safe or something, he believed, was the one dead ahead. The wall was half-angled shelves that held sneakers. About 50 pairs of them and about a dozen drawers, which he checked, feeling along the inside, searching each one for a release mechanism, but came up empty. The only things in the drawer were socks, shirts, and underwear. Drawing a blank, he took a step back from the wall.

The wall unit seemed to be one piece. Parker knew an excellent caftsman could hide anything in plain sight. He walked out of the walk-in and back into the bedroom. He looked around, dumbfounded, and sat on the bed. The remote on the end table next to the bathroom piqued his curiosity. Parker looked around the room and saw no TV or radio. It must be a hidden system. He picked up the remote. The remote looked like a piece of clear plastic. He could see straight through the damn thing. When he touched the screen with his thumb, it lit up in a bright white light.

Several bars appeared on the screen: TV, stereo, lights, and windows. Lights and windows, he thought rich people were really lazy, weren't they? He pressed the square for TV, and a concealed unit on the wall between the walk-in and the bathroom opened. It slid somewhere out of sight behind the wall. There was an entire unit behind the wall, a 40-something-inch TV, a stereo, and a DVD player. The works. He looked at the remote as more boxes appeared on the clear screen. One stood out to him. He pressed it. A second later, a box popped up requesting an access code. He pressed 1234567 until it wouldn't allow any more numbers. A moment later, ACCESS DENIED flashed on the screen in red. Something seven letters long? He tried the rich kid's name. Nothing. Parker was sure it wouldn't have anything to do with the kid himself. No. That wasn't what he'd been about. What would he use? The probable answer would be something he loved.

Was someone…

Now, that someone would either be singular or plural. And over the years, Parker got really good at crossword puzzles—a phrase popped into his head. *Mom and Dad.* The reason why the kid reached out to Parker In the first place. But it was too long, and there was no ampersand on the remote's pad. However, there was the letter N. *Fuck it,* he thought as he entered momndad and hit enter. Nothing. Not yet discouraged, he tried MomnDad. Again, nothing.

There were just too many possibilities, but without much thought, he typed in MOMNDAD. A green password accepted flashed and disappeared. The boxes now on the screen were quite interesting. There were four boxes: Security, Cameras, Panic Room, and the letter S. He pressed the last one and was rewarded with another box asking for a password. He went back to the main menu. There was no way he'd get lucky again. Out of the three remaining boxes, he pressed panic room.

Another series of boxes: open, close, view, and lockdown. Parker chose open—a loud click emanated from the closet. He went into the closet and saw dead ahead that the shelves were now skewed. He pulled it open and stepped in. The lights inside the room were already on. By the looks of the walls, the kid did indeed have guns. Weapons of all types lined the walls. He turned back to the door, and on the side, there was a handle. He pulled the door closed. Besides the guns, several flat-panel TVs hung on the walls. They all came to life when the doors shut.

The panic room became the command center—a well-equipped one at that. One of the screens displayed several boxes, so he looked at the remote. The same boxes were on there as well. An override, Parker thought it would seem the kid didn't take any chances. The panic room would also make a good hiding place if and when the cops showed up. He was sure that eventually, they would.

He sat there for a moment before deciding he better get his ass moving. First, he'd drive out to the house. It only made sense, seeing he was only a couple of towns away. He stood and searched the rooms for what he needed. After finding several magazines and a box of ammo, he left the room. He went down to the garage, where he found several expensive rides. He jumped behind the wheel of the least expensive one. A BMW 760 XI. He found the keys where he expected them to be found—in the ignition. Parker had cruised around town a lot when he first got out, the kid letting him use whichever one he'd like. Each time the keys were where he now found them. The ride out to Michael's place was quick. He knew they had no servants except a chef, who probably wasn't called in today. He wasn't that surprised when he saw the darkened house. Parker didn't bother checking more thoroughly; instead, he just drove on past, heading back to Boston.

The elevator doors dung open. Parker stepped inside, pressed the floor button, and the doors slid closed as the elevator moved upward. He stepped outside the elevator when the doors opened on the 18th floor. The law offices of Peckerwood, Asswipe, and Penis-breath occupied the entire right side of the floor and about half of the left side.

The entrance to the law firm was dead ahead at the end of a short corridor. He walked toward the law firm's double golden doors. When he was about to reach the law firm, Parker stopped and turned left to a door. The writing on the glass read Newberry Data Processing Center. A keycard reader was mounted to the left of the door. He swiped the card, the red dot turned green, and entered the office space beyond.

The office space contained five rooms. First, it opened up to a reception area. The office was dark and would remain so until 8 AM. He didn't bother turning on the lights. Instead, he crossed the expanse off the main floor and entered a room to the left of two offices with windows. He turned and walked to the office on the left.

The Data Processing Center opened two years ago and was owned by the kid. He opened it as part of the plan. Parker entered the office and sat behind the desk. The three monitors came to life with the push of the power button. On two of the screens showed images—three people were on one. The other was on but showed a black screen. Parker tapped on the keyboard and left the screen divided into six clips. The boxes showed various areas of the law firm next door. Except for the office suite, the place was dark.

Parker focused on the three people in the frame, but he wondered where the fourth person had gone. He turned up the volume to hear the conversation and stayed in front of the three screens for two hours. When Parker was satisfied, he had enough information. He reached into the desk drawer, removed an iPad connected to the office system, and left.

Three blocks away, Parker hailed a cab. The driver was perfect. When he got inside the back, he acted drunk. He gave the cabbie an address. Ten minutes later, they pulled up to a big red brick building. It was late, so the streets were exceptionally deserted. Not a soul around.

"$19.35," the driver said.

"Here, you go…my…friend," he slurred, handing the cabbie a $50 bill.

The man thought this was his lucky day. The big man in the back got out, stumbled over the curb, and fell back against the cab. He shook his head, poor bastard. Drunk or not. As much as he wanted to keep the extra money, he couldn't bring himself to rip off someone so drunk. He rolled down his window. "Excuse me?"

The big man turned toward him—his eyes glass.

"You-overpay. Too much."

"Wow," he slurred, "an honest cabbie…that's new. What did I give you?"

"A fifty-dollar bill, see," the cabbie said, holding it up.

Parker knew what he gave the driver, which was the conversation he wanted.

"Keep it," Parker said. He then turned around, stumbled, and crashed through some trash cans on the curb to the ground. The cabbie was out of the car in a second, helping Parker to his feet.

"Here, big guy, let me help you," he said. "Where you going…to that door?" Parker nodded. The cabbie helped him to the door. Parker unlocked it and entered the hallway with the aid of his newfound friend. The door closed softly behind them.

Parker walked to the first door.

"I…can…take it from here," he said with a burp. "Thank you." The cabbie made it about halfway back. "Oh, one more thing."

"What's that?" The cabbie asked, turning back. His kind face filled with fear because a gun was now pointing directly at him. The man no longer seemed drunk, but his eyes were still glass. At that moment, he knew he would not live to see his family again.

Two loud shots reverberated through the empty building's large hallway as the bullets entered through the cab driver's forehead and right cheek. The man fell heavily to the threadbare floor. Although Parker didn't need to, he hurried to swap clothes with the dead man. The building was slated for demolition, and the cabbie would have seen the large banner saying so if it wasn't still dark.

Once Parker was in the man's close, he jumped into the cab and returned to the office building where Mark and the kid were. He staked out the main entrance in plain sight at the cab stand while he watched and listened to what was going on in the office eighteen stories above. Wasn't technology great?

At about 6 AM, he saw Mark and the kid come out of the building. He pulled away from the curb, heading in their direction. Mark put up his hand. Parker pulled over to pick up the fare.

He went through the motions using his best Indian accent. Brian gave him the address. One Parker knew because he had just been there. He periodically glanced in the rearview mirror as he drove. He even tried to strike up a conversation with no success. Of course, this was fine by him. Parker saw no recognition on their faces—as far as Mark was concerned, he was dead, which was a good thing.

The plan was to drive out toward Brian's house and pretend to get lost. He'd blame the GPS or something, and then he would pull over.... Hopefully, he could get them distracted. Maybe with a map or something. While they were occupied, he'd slipped out to use the bathroom but would actually be going where he left his car. His exit approached. *Showtime.*

35

CAR RIDE

The taxi turned left onto Tremont, moving with the typical Boston traffic. Mark and Brian engaged in conversation. They barely paid attention, if at all, to the changing scenery beyond the car's windows. When they were out of town, the cab driver interrupted the conversation to ask if they preferred him to take the pike and told them it would save a little bit of time. Mark told the driver that it was okay. A few moments later, they were moving briskly along I90, heading West to the town of Needham.

The driver started having problems with the GPS. He smacked it on the side—the loud smacking sound made Brian jump. The driver noticed Brian's eyes peering at him through the rearview.

"So…sorry. This thing give me problem…all day," the cab driver said with a thick faux-Indian accent. "I pull over to try and fix. Okay?"

Mark looked around. They had pulled off I90 a few minutes back. "You know where you are?" He asked Brian. "Does anything look familiar?"

Brian looked at Mark and nodded. "Yeah, kinda, but we're still really far from my house."

"Can you direct him to your house from here?"

Brian looked out both sides of the windows and glanced out the front. "No, I don't think so. Besides, I take the train to downtown or call a cab."

"Spoiled, I tell you," Mark said with a laugh and then to the cabbie. "Yeah, go ahead."

The car pulled over to the side of the road. Mark couldn't see a house anywhere. The isolation made him nervous— and his trustworthy intuition started to ring the alarm. Quietly at first, but enough for Mark to keep a watchful eye on what the cabbie was doing. The man held the Garmin GPS unit in his hand. He pressed the touchscreen's buttons before placing it back on the dashboard.

"Did you get it working?"

"No, the screen froze up. It says we are still in Boston. First Dedham, now Boston. The thing is…I don't know…crazy."

"Just drive," Mark said. "We'll find it."

"Pay attention, little man, and tell me when you're familiar enough with the area to get us to the house?"

"Sure, if I can."

The cabbie looked back at them. "You recognize the area?" Then he shook his head. "No—you don't, do you? I drive now. What's near your house?"

"I know my way from the Needham Heights Plaza. I don't think we're in Needham yet. A street approached, and the street's name looked familiar to Brian. "Take this right. I think this will lead to my neighborhood."

The cabbie smiled. Quick. Mark almost missed it. He also saw recognition. The guy knew where he was going. He better not be trying to squeeze more money out of them—that ain't happening.

"I hope that meter stopped running back when your GPS went nuts?"

"No, we still run. You should know where you go."

"Yeah, that's funny. Because I think you know where you are—pull over."

The man's eyes got wide.

"Don't worry. You gotta have a map in here, right?"

"Sure, in the glove box. I think there is one," the cabbie said as he pulled over. But it's a big one."

The cabbie put the car in park, reached into the glove compartment, pulled out a map, and handed it back to them. Mark unfolded it, temporarily blocking out the cabbie. The driver's side door opened, and the cabbie started to exit. Mark folded down the map.

"I go take a leak, okay," he said, motioning to the side of the road. "Okay?"

"Yeah, whatever," he said, looking back at the map. "Okay, little man, where are we?"

He kept his non-trusting eyes on the cabbie as he talked.

"Right there," Brian said smugly. "My house is here."

"Shit, really, it's only a few miles away. And it looks like you're right. Where not in Needham and won't be for another mile. The cabbie walked back to the cab and opened Brian's door.

"You find?"

"Yeah, only a couple miles."

"Good. Good. We go now," The cabbie said, shutting the door and walking around to the driver's side.

The map still blocked some of their view. "All right, can you get us there? Think you can handle that, Lil man?"

"No problem."

"Good," Mark said, pushing the top of the map down to see. "Where'd he Go?"

Mark's internal alarm started blaring—something wasn't right. He looked out the front and side windows. No sign of the cabbie. *Fuck*, he cursed himself.

"Get out the car!" He said, pushing Brian toward the passenger side door.

"What?"

"Come on, open the door," he said, remembering the cabbie had opened Brian's door. "No, not that way."

He tried to open his door. Locked. Fuck! Cover your face."

"Why?"

"Just do it."

Mark swung to the left, bringing his knees toward his chest—then, with all the power he could muster, he thrust both feet toward the window. Safety glass rained down onto the seat and floor. He quickly cleared the window of any debris. As he climbed out, he urged Brian to follow.

"Come on, but stay behind me, and be careful of the glass."

"Okay," Brian said, his voice trembling a bit. Fear hijacking his vocal cords once again. "Where's…the…cabbie?"

Mark climbed fully out and turned back to help Brian. He half climbed out the window, hugging Mark around the neck as Mark pulled him from the car. Brian still clung to him as the big man ran across the deserted street. Mark scanned the area. Not a house in sight. On the other side of the road, he could see it pitch downward into a ditch. They started down the steep grade.

A bright white-hot light engulfed them as a powerful invisible force pushed them into the gravel-filled ditch. Mark hit the ground, sprawled face-first into the pit. Pain erupted throughout his body and moaned in agony. His eyes involuntarily shut from the pain. He forced them open. Brian lay a few feet away on his back, grimacing from the pain he felt.

"You okay?" Mark asked.

"Yeah, I think so, but my head hurts."

Due to the pain, Mark crawled slowly back up the embankment to check out the scene. Every Injury he incurred that day lit up all at once. The cab was engulfed in flames. The air reeked of burning metal and vinyl. A retching smell. He searched the area for the cabbie, but there was no sign of the man. He looked up the street. Nothing. Then back the way they had come.

A car slowly approached.

Mark suppressed the urge to run into the street. The car slowed down before he pulled over behind the burning vehicle. A man got out, but Mark could not see the man's face, but he had a cellphone pressed to his ear. Mark could hear the man talking on the cellphone. "There's a burning car. A cab, I think. No, I don't think so—they couldn't possibly be alive."

The man said a few more things before hanging up the cellphone and putting it back in his pocket. The flames abated some. The man cautiously approached the vehicle. He appeared to be trying to see if anybody was inside the car.

The man stood up straight and appeared to be looking off into the woods beyond the car. He spun slowly, looking off into the distance. When his gaze met Mark's, there was a sense of recognition. The man wore a dark-colored coat, but underneath was a bright-colored shirt that matched the one the cabbie wore. The cabbie wasn't an accomplice—it was Parker. Parker turned, smiling, and headed back toward the burning car.

Mark made his move—rushing out of the ditch and across the street. Parker never heard him coming before he was tackled to the ground. Mark landed thunderous blows to Parker's side. Parker gained the upper hand after kicking Mark in the side of the head with his instep, momentarily dazing Mark and making him step back.

Parker scrambled to his feet and threw a powerful roundhouse kick to Mark's side. Mark recovered in time to swing up and catch the kick in his chest while simultaneously grabbing Parker's leg and using his momentum to bring him crashing down onto his back. Air swooshed from his lungs. Mark quickly twisted around and struck his chin. Then again, with the other fist.

Mark lunged forward with an elbow to the side of Parker's head. Parker didn't move. Mark checked his pulse. Faint but still alive. He swung himself under Parker, wrapped his arm around Parker's neck, and started to squeeze.

"Don't!" Brian cried. "Don't do it."

Mark glanced at Brian, who was running toward him. Brian stopped, tears rolling down his face. Mark's anger subsided, and he released the man. Brian ran to Mark as he got to his feet and hugged him.

"I'm sorry," he said to Brian.

"I know. I know."

They were still near Parker's unconscious body. The fire raged while sirens off in the distance added to the fire's snap, crackle, and pop of the blaze. Mark looked down at Parker; the fire spread toward the man.

"Well, I guess we better pull him away from the fire, then."

Brian looked at Parker lying unconscious but said nothing.

Mark grabbed Parker by his wrist and dragged him to his parked car. A small explosion cracked from somewhere in the fire. The fire brightened briefly. Sirens got louder. Mark could see a cruiser approaching with its lights flashing. For once, he wasn't nervous at the sight of one.

Brian clung to his side as the cruiser pulled over. Two uniform officers got out.

"Was he in that?" The first cop asked, shaking his head.

"No," Mark said. "We were."

Mark and Brian moved away from Parker.

"What happened?" The other cop asked.

"Now, that's a long story."

"He tried to kill us," Brian stated dramatically.

The officers laughed.

Movement behind Mark made him spin. Parker was no longer unconscious. He was now on his knees with a Glock held tightly in his right hand. Mark stepped in front of Brian and into the path of the gun. Parker squeezed the trigger, hitting Mark twice in the abdomen. He fell to his knees as the officers drew their weapons and shot Parker—killing him.

36

REDEMPTION ROAD

The Lamborghini navigated smoothly along the boulevard as its powerful V12 engine rumbled and whined beneath them. Mark downshifted, bringing the beast to a more acceptable speed. Brian sat shotgun, enjoying the ride. Things finally went back to some kind of normality. If him driving a $300,000 Italian sports car could somehow be considered normal even though it was a rental.

Brian's 13th birthday present.

They had the luxury sports car for a week. Although Mark suspected it was as much for him as the kid, it was what Brian wanted. Brian knew the Aventador was his favorite sports car. He slowed the car down as he approached the next intersection. Brian's school was a block ahead. The light turned red.

Boston was a resilient city, and it rebounded quickly. Mark believed most thought about the attack as they rode public transportation, which was to be expected. Doubtful, he'd ride a train again without being hyper-vigilant. His life could not be any better. Even though he was a glorified babysitter, it could have been much worse, right? He knew it could. The light changed, and he crossed the intersection. He turned to Brian as he lowered the radio.

"You ready for superstar status?"

"Of course, but Ricky gets dropped off in a Rolls Royce."

"I'm not sure, but this isn't too shabby, my friend."

He pulled over to the curb in front of the school. The kids in front of the school took notice.

"See, it still gets its respect."

Brian smiled. "I guess it does," he said, swinging up the door. "See you later."

"I'll think about it, Just kidding, Lil man. When I pick you up, I'll give you my birthday gift, alright?"

Before he stopped, Brian was halfway out of the car and turned to look at Mark. "I still don't know why you won't give it to me now?"

"Because I don't have it with me now."

"Funny. It better be good."

"I'm sure you'll like it," he said. "Now get your butt moving to class."

"All right," he said with a bit of a whine.

Mark watched Brian get surrounded by some of his classmates as the Lambo's door closed. Mark knew they were asking questions about the ride. Brian moved a few more feet toward the school, turned, and waved. Mark returned the gesture. The smile on Brian's face was priceless. The kid could have anything in the world, but he chose something he thought Mark would like. Brian made it to the building's double doors and disappeared beyond. Satisfied, Brian was safe; he pulled away from the curb. Mark made it a block when his cellphone beeped. He received a text message. He picked up the phone and read the message.

Everyone is like, OMG… That's a Lambo! You were right.

He smiled and laughed.

Mark had several errands to do before heading back to the house. Life was good. Nice and quiet, just the way he liked it. If the road to redemption was long, he was just turning onto the street.

The first stop was an out-of-the-way computer shop near MIT that technophiles liked. The store carried cool tech gadgets, but they also did upgrades to computers and phones. He needed to update the GPS program on his laptop and iPhone. He stole an idea from Parker's playbook. Every pair of sneakers Brian wears has a GPS tracker inside them, but those were for backup. The central unit hung around his neck. The first thank you gift he had given his charge. A white gold and diamond lion pendant. The kid never took it off.

As he parked the car to go into the computer shop, he thought about the look he was sure to get when Mark brought Brian his gift. His friend Kevin was visiting from out West, and Mark arranged for him to get a helicopter to take them on a private tour. The kid deserved the best birthday after what he went through. People say nothing could repay Mark for what he did for Brian, but the truth was he didn't save Brian—Brian saved him. He got out, crossed the street, and went into the shop.

# # # #

Brian stood by his locker between classes. He needed to get his advanced calculus textbook for the next class. His day couldn't get any better. Everyone got dropped off in Mercedes, BMW, and Lexus, but it was the price of going to an exclusive prep school like Tilden Academy.

The school was located just outside of Boston. Most of the students lived on campus. A few did not—those who lived in the area. Regardless of money, only a few got dropped off in Rolls Royces, Bently's, or Maybachs. He'd never thought getting dropped off in an exotic sports car had its own class. He grabbed his book and shut his locker.

Someone playfully pushed him into the locker door— and punched him in the arm thirteen times. He turned. It was his friend Ricky. The kid who got dropped off in the Rolls Royce. "Happy Birthday, Brian."

Brian punched him back. "Whatever. I'll remember your birthday when it comes."

Ricky stepped back and put up his hands in surrender. "Okay, okay. You got that."

"You ready for the calculus test today."

"No, not really."

Brian shook his head.

"So, was that you getting dropped off in a Lambo," Ricky said with a smile. "Let me find out you been holding out on me."

"Nah, it's rented. I got it for a week."

"That's cool."

A couple of the other kids passing by said Happy Birthday

and commented on the ride. He was surprised that the Lambo was a big hit in a school where everyone seemed to pride themselves more on qualities than bank accounts.

The school taught them to focus on qualities such as honesty, loyalty, and respect.

But then again, if one could afford to spend that kind of money on something as ostentatious as a sports car, they somehow fit right in step with the rest of the power born. Even in his school, there was an elite crowd.

"Hey, what are you doing after school?" Ricky asked as they walked to room 272 for homeroom.

"Well, I'm not sure," Mark said something about a plan, but I don't know what. Why?"

"Oh, nothing. I thought you could come over to my house. My dad's away on a business trip, but my mom's home, and she likes it when I have friends over. Besides, it would only be until your party, anyway. It's at seven, right?"

"Yeah, but I'm sorry, but I can't come over today," Brian said as they entered the classroom. "Hey, how about you come with me today. I'm sure Mark won't mind."

"I know you told me, and I get that he saved your life, but I don't get why you hang out with your driver like he's a friend of something. He's your driver."

"True, but when he saved my life, he didn't know me at all—should tell you something about the type of person he is."

Brian hated when people talked down about Mark like he was just something paid for—he was family.

"Oh, no. Don't get me wrong, Mark's cool. I never had that kind of connection with someone that worked for us.

They walked to their desks, which were side-by-side.

Ricky's desk was on the right. He leaned toward Brian in a conspiratorial tone he asked. "Did he really spend time in prison?"

"Um, yeah, like eight years."

"He's really tough, huh?"

"I guess."

Ricky glanced back to the back of the room where one of his bodyguards was standing. One stayed with him wherever he went. The other stayed outside in the car. They were in constant contact with each other. It was the price of what his father did for work. His father was the CEO of a multinational company with connections in many government communities throughout the world. The only place he got freedom was at home. It was the only place his bodyguards disappeared into the woodwork.

He nodded toward his bodyguard. "Tougher than my BGs?"

Brian smiled. "Hands down."

###

Mark headed home after getting his ass handed to him on the chessboard. He lost before, but eight out of ten was really bad. He felt the kid barely out of his teens was taking it easy on him. He checked his watch. There was plenty of time before he had to meet the party planner. There would be a hundred guests at Brian's Birthday celebration, and that was just the kids.

These days birthday parties are as much an adult affair. There would also be a lot of security. Primarily because of Brian's best friend, Ricky. The kid's family was mega-rich and had been targeted several times by extremist groups on both sides of the world. Because of the security risk, the party would be held at the mansion in Needham. Mark had the best system money could buy installed and personally swept daily for devices that did not belong.

He pulled into the private driveway as the party planner arrived. She had come highly recommended. They had already met her once before. She was expensive but knowledgeable about such things as teenagers' birthday parties. He motioned to her to follow him up to the house. Mark parked out front, and the party planner pulled up behind him and parked. They got out of their vehicles.

He approached her.

"Mark, right?" she asked, reaching out her hand.

Taking her hand: "Yes," he said, flashing a friendly smile. "Follow me, and I'll show you to the rooms we will be using for the party."

"Have all the guests confirmed?"

"As far as we know, there will be 300, including parents and security but a hundred kids."

"Well, we better get started then," she said as they walked into the house.

###

During seventh period, the last class of the day, Brian couldn't hold it any longer; he needed to use the bathroom. Bad. But he didn't want to miss anything in class. Computers-3 was an advanced class he really liked. It was one of his favorites, and he hated to miss any of it. So, he was now in the boys' restroom, trying to hurry along his bodily functions. He finished, washed his hands, and headed back to class.

Nobody was in the hallway.

A door to one of the classrooms opened, and two men dressed in suits exited the room with a boy sandwiched between them. Immediately, he recognized one of the guards and the boy—Ricky. He wondered what was going on. He stopped as they headed toward him, and when they passed, he asked Ricky if everything was okay.

Ricky tried to stop, but one of his bodyguards pushed him forward, "We need to go, Richard," he said with urgency.

Sorry, but I gotta go, he mouthed back to Brian.

Brian saw confusion in his friend's eyes and something else he believed to be fear. Ricky being dragged out of school by his bodyguards wasn't exactly a new thing. As a matter of fact, it happened quite often. At least every other week or so. Brian still worried as he watched his friend go to the doors to the stairwell and disappear.

He was glad it wasn't him. Having around-the-clock security and threats against his family and stuff—was too much on a kid. However, he hoped his friend was okay, and he was able to make it to his party. Although somehow Brian doubted Ricky would be available, he still hoped he could come.

He stood in the empty hallway for a moment before returning to class.

As it turned out, Brian got lucky and hadn't missed much at all. He finished working on the program he was writing. He was learning how to design websites and digital cartoons using various code. It was cool. Class ended, and the school day with it. The bell rang, and he followed the crowd of students out of the building.

The Lamborghini waited at the curb with Mark behind the wheel. A small crowd, some friends, and some hangers-on gathered around Brian as he walked to his ride.

Once inside, he buckled up in the passenger seat and smiled gleefully at Mark.

"Had a good day…did you, now?"

"Sure did," he replied, then thought about his friend. "But I don't think Ricky's gonna make it to my party."

"Oh, too bad, I like that kid," he said. "He ain't a snob like some of your other friends…but whatta bout that girl Jen, is she coming?"

"Sure is," he said with a big ole cheese grin. "She told me today. I'm so happy right now, but I think the Lambo did it. Everyone kept asking if they could take a ride in it. I told them it was up to you because it only seats two people, and you'll have to drive."

"I don't know about taking a hundred kids for a ride, but we can let them climb in and check it out."

"Yeah, when you put it that way, I wouldn't want to do it either," he said, "so where're we going?"

"I'm taking you to your birthday gift," Mark said with a smirk, not giving any hint. "My friend Kevin is waiting on us. Hey, before I forget, what happened with Ricky? They pulled him out again?"

"Yeah, wouldn't even let me talk to him to see what's going on."

"Well, I saw on the news that his father was in London at some conference. If you want, I'll call his mom and see if he can still come. Maybe even use my 15 seconds of fame or something. You know, like: "Hey, someone tried to blow up Brian like twenty times, and he's still alive."

"Wasn't it like nine…"

Mark held up a finger to his lips. "Shhh, my secret."

Brian laughed and stomped his right foot.

"Careful now. That section of the car's worth about 60 grand."

Brian laughed more.

Mark called Ricky's house; his mother answered but couldn't talk for long. She didn't have time to explain what had happened. Her husband had gotten another threat to his family's lives. So, as they often do, they decided to play it safe. She didn't think Ricky could make it to the party, but she sounded disappointed that he couldn't and wished Brian a Happy Birthday. She even, in the end, let Ricky talk to his best friend.

Ricky told Brian he was sorry he couldn't come, but he would if there were a way he could. Ricky's mother told him he had to get off the phone; Brian told Ricky he could call him on his cellphone if he needed anything. Then Brian hung up the phone as they pulled into the heliport.

Brian took in the five helicopters lined up in a row. "Are we going up in one of those?"

"We sure are," Mark said as he spotted his friend and pilot, Kevin.

He pulled into a parking spot next to his friend's car, and they got out.

"Nice ride," Kevin said. "I see you're doing all right, now, huh?"

"It's a rental," he said, motioning to Brian. "One of his birthday presents."

"And I am the other, cool," Kevin said. "But now that I see that…you know… I'm gonna want to take a ride, even as a passenger would be fine."

"Yeah, you got that; let's fly."

The three of them walked to the helipad with an excellent bird resting on it. The Robison R47 was a small but efficient helicopter. Brian's bright eyes and smiling face told Mark it was all worth it.

They were up in the air for 20 minutes when Brian's phone rang. He answered it, but he had trouble hearing, so Brian checked the screen. Ricky. He hoped his friend could hear him tell him about the helicopter, but he couldn't hear very well himself. He listened, still nothing but muffled sounds. *Must have pocket-dialed me*, he thought before hanging up. A moment later, the cellphone dinged. The notification for a text. He read the short message, and it scared him. "Mark! We…I mean…Ricky…has a problem," Brian said into his headset.

Mark turned back, and Brian handed him the phone. He read the text message.

I'm in the trunk. HELP! New BG. Not good. HELP! HELP!

Mark showed Kevin the text.

"Is that real?"

"I believe so."

"So, what do you want to do?"

"Let's go get him."

"Roger that."

Mark texted back: *Hang tight.*

The bird changed course and headed toward Ricky's mansion.

AUTHOR NOTE

November 1, 2022

Dear Constant Reader,

I have only a couple of titles out and more to come, and I thank you for coming along for the ride. It has been a long 7 years since Something Wicked was published.

The current title, which still holds the same themes as my other works, is my favorite novel so far, and to watch the book morph and change over the years was a lesson well worth the struggle.

Initially written in 2006, my publisher and I put it on hold because of the Boston Bombing. Once the movie came out, the process of updating the novel began, which is now set closer to now. In hindsight, I wish I had decided to keep it set back then, but the challenge intrigued me, and I am pleased with the results.

Mark and Brian had one hell of a journey, and I was happy that both survived. I wasn't so sure they would.

Initially, this novel was written as a standalone, and the following books in the series will also be standalone, so you can pick up whichever story appeals to you. I write gritty tales, and I know my novels aren't for everyone. But I believe in redemption and love antihero stories and found a publisher who not only focuses on disenfranchised authors but prison lit and antihero stories as much as I do.

I am grateful to all of you. Now please understand I am not the best writer and never claim to be, but I think I did one hell of a job here. It is my best work so far, but you faithful reader will be the judge as you share and leave reviews as to how well or awful you felt I did—and either is just fine with me because providing you the best experience is my first and foremost aim.

I hope Mark Toren met your standards and deserves redemption. As many of you know, I write crime because crime is what I know fits who I am. An influx of constant change. I want those incarcerated and who have already come home to know that they too can be the hero of their own story—who doesn't like the books or movies where the rebel or outlaw is the hero. Surrounded by archetypes of many crime novels, I threw my hat in the game and made a career.

Thank you again for taking this ride with me, and I hope to eventually get to meet some of you, and please send me fan mail. Hell, it doesn't need to be fan mail. If you have complaints or suggestions, shoot them over to me. I will grow as a writer from the input you give.

Cheers,
John A Galeotto

ABOUT THE AUTHOR

John A Galeotto is a 3rd generation Italian American mixed with who knows how many other ethnicities.

He grew up on the streets and has worked as a hip-hop promoter, a rapper, a store clerk (multiple times), an inmate worker (several times), Specialty retail as a store concept designer, and a drug dealer before going on a long vacation.

He writes crime thrillers that sometimes, more often than not, blend with other genres. He lives in Boston, MA, where he is working on many novels to come.

Lightning Source UK Ltd.
Milton Keynes UK
UKHW012238060223
416577UK00010B/777/J